Grade
2

Math for the Gifted Student

Challenging Activities for the Advanced Learner

Written by **Kathy Furgang**

Illustrations by **Clive Scruton**

An imprint of Sterling Children's Books

FLASH KIDS, STERLING, and the distinctive Sterling logo are registered trademarks of
Sterling Publishing Co., Inc.

Published by Sterling Publishing Co., Inc.
387 Park Avenue South, New York, NY 10016
Text and illustrations © 2005 by Flash Kids
Distributed in Canada by Sterling Publishing
c/o Canadian Manda Group, 165 Dufferin Street
Toronto, Ontario, Canada M6K 3H6
Distributed in the United Kingdom by GMC Distribution Services
Castle Place, 166 High Street, Lewes, East Sussex, England BN7 1XU
Distributed in Australia by Capricorn Link (Australia) Pty. Ltd.
P.O. Box 704, Windsor, NSW 2756, Australia

Sterling ISBN 978-1-4114-3434-9

Manufactured in Canada

Lot #:
6 8 10 9 7 5
12/12

For information about custom editions, special sales, premium and
corporate purchases, please contact Sterling Special Sales
Department at 800-805-5489 or specialsales@sterlingpublishing.com.

Cover image © SW Productions/Getty Images
Cover design and production by Mada Design, Inc.

If you find that your child is unchallenged

by traditional workbooks and math practice drills, this workbook will provide the stimulation your student has been looking for. This workbook contains much more than typical second-grade drill pages and questions; it does not rely on the assumption that a gifted second grader simply requires third-grade work. The logic-based activities cover the national math standards for second grade while also providing kids with a chance to grow and challenge themselves beyond the work they do in the regular classroom. This workbook covers the curriculum areas of number sense, operations and computations, patterns, money, logical thinking, measurement, geometry, graphing, probability, and statistics.

Encourage your student to use models or scrap paper to work out problems or to help him or her work through more difficult activities. Allow your student to skip around and do activities that interest him or her. The activities in the book encourage independent thinking and stimulate creativity. Your student can check his or her answers by using the answer key at the end of the book.

By utilizing this workbook series, you are providing your gifted learner an opportunity to experience scholastic achievement at an advanced level, thereby fostering confidence and an increased desire to learn.

Stand in Order

Students in the school parade must march in order from the smallest number to the greatest number. The order the children should march in is written on their shirts. Circle the number in each group that is out of order. Then draw a line to the place it belongs in the line.

1.

2.

3.

4.

Making Numbers

Use these balloons to make three-digit numbers. There are six different numbers that can be made. Write them in the balloons below.

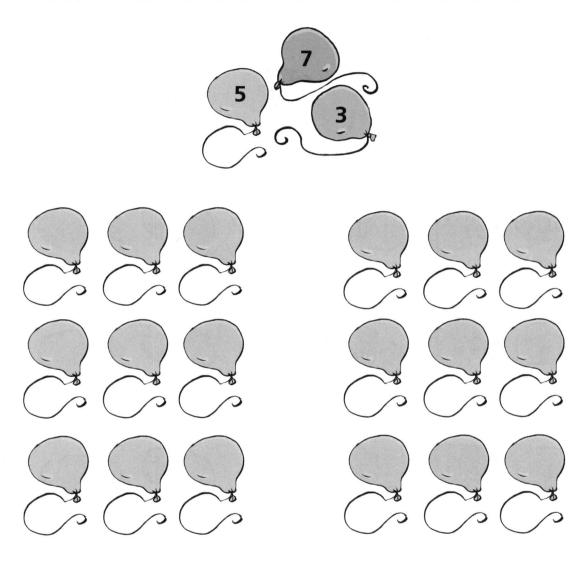

Write the numbers in order from greatest to least.

_____, _____, _____, _____, _____, _____

Lily Pads

Figure out the pattern in each row of lily pads below.
Then finish the pattern.

1.

101   103   105   107

2.

450   445   440   435

3.

203   206   209   212

4.

331   341   351   361

5.

722   724   726   728

Make 75 Cents

Using the coins below, write six different ways to make 75 cents.
Each coin can be used more than once.

1.
2.
3.
4.
5.
6.

7. If you have only nickels, how many would you need to equal 75 cents? _____

Both Numbers and Words

Answer each question by writing the number and the word.

1. What number has 3 thousands, 4 hundreds, 0 tens, and 8 ones?

Write the number. _____ Write the word. _____

_____

2. What number has 7 hundreds, 8 tens, and 3 ones?

Write the number. _____ Write the word. _____

_____

3. What number has 9 thousands, 0 hundreds, 7 tens, and no ones?

Write the number. _____ Write the word. _____

_____

4. What number has 6 hundreds, 3 tens, and 9 ones?

Write the number. _____ Write the word. _____

_____

5. What number has 1 thousand, 1 hundred, 3 tens, and 3 ones?

Write the number. _____ Write the word. _____

_____

6. What number has 4 hundreds, 2 tens, and 8 ones?

Write the number. _____ Write the word. _____

_____

So Many Hats

The hat store must put hats on the shelf in order by number. The number is written on each hat. Circle the number that is out of order.
Then draw a line to the place it belongs in the line.

1. 408 412 410 406 404 402

2. 749 736 777 729 710 707

3. 189 131 174 160 154 148

4. 398 381 368 359 348 379

Bird Numbers

These birds can stand together to make three-digit numbers.
There are six different numbers that the birds can make.
Write the numbers in the birds below.

Write the numbers in order from least to greatest.

_____, _____, _____, _____, _____, _____

Make 80 Cents

Using the coins below, draw six different ways to make 80 cents.
Each coin can be used more than once.

1.	
2.	
3.	
4.	
5.	
6.	

Lost and Found

Answer the questions below.

Markie found money under the cushions of the couch.
This is what he found.

1. How much money did Markie find? _____

2. Markie also found money under the cushions of a chair. He found the same amount of money, but only 5 coins. Draw the coins Markie found under the chair cushions.

3. Of all the money Markie found, he gave his sister all of the quarters. How many quarters did he give his sister? _____

4. How much money did Markie have left after he gave the quarters to his sister? _____

More or Less?

Count the coins below to see who has more money.

Mike

1. Mike has _____ cents.

Joleen

2. Joleen has _____ cents.

Rebecca

3. Rebecca has _____ cents.

4. Who has the most money? _____

5. Who has the least money? _____

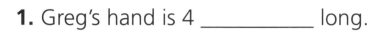

Which Unit of Length?

Write **inches, feet,** or **yards** to complete each sentence below. Choose the unit of length that makes the most sense.

1. Greg's hand is 4 _____ long.

2. Mr. Lang's rake is 4 _____ long.

3. Britney's key is 1 _____ long.

4. Dave's car is 7 _____ long.

5. Lori's television is 2 _____ long.

6. List three things that are <u>about</u> the same length as a magazine.

_____

_____

_____

Feet or Yards?

Write **feet** or **yards** to tell the best way to measure each object.

1.

_____

2.

_____

3.

_____

4.

_____

5.

_____

6.

_____

7.

_____

8.

_____

What Time Is It?

Look at the time on each wall clock.
Then write the time on each alarm clock.

1.

2.

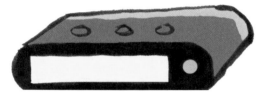

3.

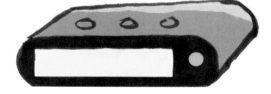

4.

5.

6.

Compare How Long

Read each task. Make a check mark by the task that you think takes longer to do. Then use a clock with a second hand to time yourself doing each task. Write whether your guess was **correct** or **incorrect** on the line.

1. ☐ Write your name.

   ☐ Turn around 5 times.

   My guess was _____.

2. ☐ Draw a square.

   ☐ Cut a paper circle.

   My guess was _____.

3. ☐ Eat a cracker.

   ☐ Write your address.

   My guess was _____.

4. ☐ Clap 20 times.

   ☐ Blink 10 times.

   My guess was _____.

Pick Up the Objects

What shape would be on the bottom of each object if you picked it up?
Draw the shape on the line. (Hint: choose from a circle, square,
or rectangle!)

1.

_____

2.

_____

3.

_____

4.

_____

5.

_____

6.

_____

Which Does Not Belong?

Look at each group of shapes. Circle the one that does not belong. Then write why it does not belong on the line.

1.

_____

2.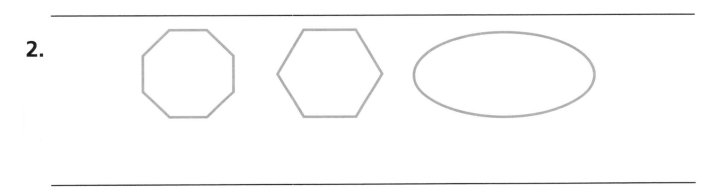

_____

3.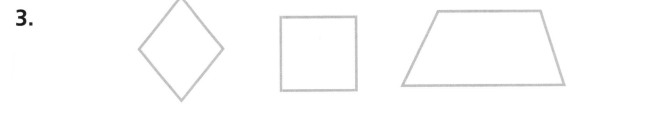

_____

4.

_____

Train Pattern

Jerry put his trains in a pattern on the floor. Figure out the patterns.
Then solve the problems.

1. Jerry lined up 10 trains. Some were blue and some were red. He
placed the trains so that every fourth one was red. Color the trains
to show the pattern.

How many trains were red? _____

How many trains were blue? _____

2. Jerry lined up 8 trains. The first train was blue and every other
train after it was blue. The rest were red. Color the trains to show
the pattern.

How many trains were red? _____

How many trains were blue? _____

3. Jerry lined up 9 trains. Every third train was red. The rest were
blue. Color the trains to show the pattern.

How many trains were red? _____

How many trains were blue? _____

Continue the Pattern

Jenny lined up her hair clips. Figure out the patterns she used.
Then answer the questions.

1.

If Jenny laid out four more clips, what would the color of the last
one be? _____

2.

If Jenny continued the pattern, what color would the 15th hair clip
be? _____

3.

If Jenny continued the pattern, how many yellow clips would be in
the next group of 12 clips? _____

4.

If Jenny continued the pattern, would the 14th clip be blue or
purple? _____

Colorful Fractions

Look at each shape. Write the fraction that describes the amount each shape is colored.

1. 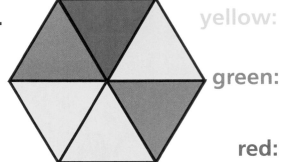 red: ⬜ blue: ⬜

2. 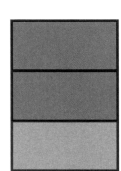 yellow: ⬜ purple: ⬜

3. 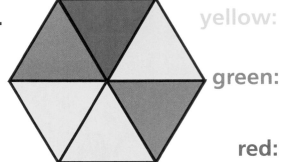 yellow: ⬜ green: ⬜ red: ⬜

4. gray: ⬜ blue: ⬜

5. 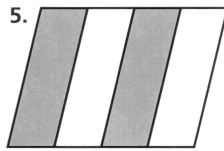 white: ⬜ orange: ⬜

6. 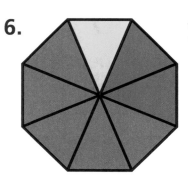 yellow: ⬜ blue: ⬜ red: ⬜

Fraction Shapes

Color each shape to show the correct fraction.

1. Color $\frac{3}{5}$ green. Color $\frac{2}{5}$ red.

2. Color $\frac{4}{8}$ yellow. Color $\frac{2}{8}$ blue. Color $\frac{2}{8}$ green.

3. Color $\frac{1}{4}$ blue. Color $\frac{3}{4}$ yellow.

4. Color $\frac{1}{3}$ orange. Color $\frac{2}{3}$ blue.

5. Color $\frac{2}{4}$ purple. Color $\frac{2}{4}$ red.

6. Color $\frac{1}{5}$ orange. Color $\frac{2}{5}$ green. Color $\frac{2}{5}$ purple.

Who Can Buy It?

Monica, Wilson, and Jake want to buy a hot dog for $1.20. Only one of them has enough money to buy it. Fill in the amounts of money that each of them have. Then determine who has enough to buy a hot dog.

1. Monica has _____.

2. Wilson has _____.

3. Jake has _____.

4. _____ can buy the hot dog.

At the Fair

Solve the problems below.

1. Today, 54 people rode the Ferris wheel and 25 people rode the carousel. How many people rode the rides in all? _____

2. The Ferris wheel turns 14 times before it stops. The carousel turns 15 times before it stops. How many times do the two rides turn in all? _____

3. There are 24 people in line for cotton candy. There are 13 people in line for popcorn. How many people in all are in line for these foods? _____

4. Four people can ride in one roller-coaster car. There are four cars in each roller coaster. How many people can ride in a roller coaster?
_____

What Is the Sign?

Write **+** or **−** in the circles to make the number sentences true. The number sentences should be read from left to right.

1. 7 ◯ 2 ◯ 3 = 6

2. 12 ◯ 2 ◯ 5 = 15

3. 4 ◯ 8 ◯ 8 = 20

4. 9 ◯ 5 ◯ 6 = 10

5. 18 ◯ 8 ◯ 3 = 7

6. 13 ◯ 4 ◯ 2 = 15

7. 20 ◯ 5 ◯ 6 = 19

8. 14 ◯ 8 ◯ 9 = 15

Apple Math

Look at each set of numbers. Use the numbers in the apples to fill in the blanks in the problems. Use each number only once in a problem.

1.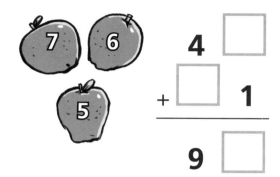

```
    4 □              □ □
 + □ 1            + 2 2
 ─────            ─────
    9 □              8 □
```

2.

```
  □ 8              1 7
 + 6 □           + □ □
 ─────           ─────
  □ 9              3 □
```

3.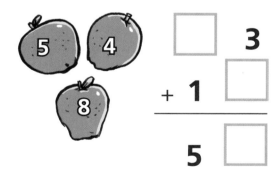

```
  □ 3              2 □
 + 1 □           + □ 4
 ─────           ─────
  5 □              7 □
```

4.

```
    7 □              □ □
 + □ 2            + 2 0
 ─────            ─────
    □ 9              □ 2
```

The Missing Shape

Figure out each pattern below. Then draw the missing shape in the pattern.

1.

2.

3.

4.

5.

6.

Write the Rule

Figure out each pattern below. Then write the rule for the pattern.

1.

What is the rule of the pattern? _____

2.

What is the rule of the pattern? _____

3.

What is the rule of the pattern? _____

4.

What is the rule of the pattern? _____

5.

What is the rule of the pattern? _____

What Time?

Answer each question by writing and drawing the time on both clocks.

1. It is 4:30. Mom will be home in 45 minutes. When will Mom be home?

2. Dad will take June to the movies in 2 and a half hours. It is 2:00. What time will Dad take June to the movies?

3. It is 3:30. Lance just finished his homework. He started it 45 minutes ago. When did Lance start his homework?

4. It has been raining for 1 hour and 15 minutes. It is now 5:00. When did it start raining?

Write the Time

Read the times below.
Then draw the hands on each clock to show the time.

1. The time is a quarter after 12.

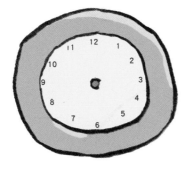

2. The time is thirty minutes after seven.

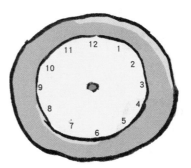

3. The time is ten minutes to nine.

4. The time is twenty minutes to three.

5. The time is twenty minutes past eleven.

6. The time is a quarter to six.

31

Pounds or Ounces?

Write **pounds** or **ounces** to tell the best way to weigh each object.

1.  _____

2.  _____

3.  _____

4.  _____

5.  _____

6.  _____

7.  _____

8.  _____

What Grade Are They In?

Susie, Sandy, and Carrie are sisters. They are each in a different grade in school. Use the clues in the box below to find out which grade each girl is in. Fill in the chart to help you.

Susie is not in first grade.

Sandy is not in second grade.

Carrie is not in third grade.

The sister whose name does not begin with an **S** is in first grade.

	First Grade	Second Grade	Third Grade
Susie			
Sandy			
Carrie			

1. Who is in first grade? _____

2. Who is in second grade? _____

3. Who is in third grade? _____

Fish, Fish!

Solve the problems.

1. There are twice as many brown fish in the pond as there are orange fish. There are 7 orange fish in the pond. How many total fish are in the pond? _____

2. A brown fish in the pond eats 3 times a day. An orange fish in the pond eats twice as many times as the brown fish. How many times in a day will the two fish be eating? _____

3. A fish in the pond sleeps for 3 hours each day. How many hours will the fish sleep in 7 days? _____

4. An orange fish swims 5 times around the pond. A brown fish swims 3 times more around the pond. How many times does the brown fish swim around the pond? _____

Hidden Addition

Find the answer to each equation in the hidden picture.
Then use the color code to color the picture.

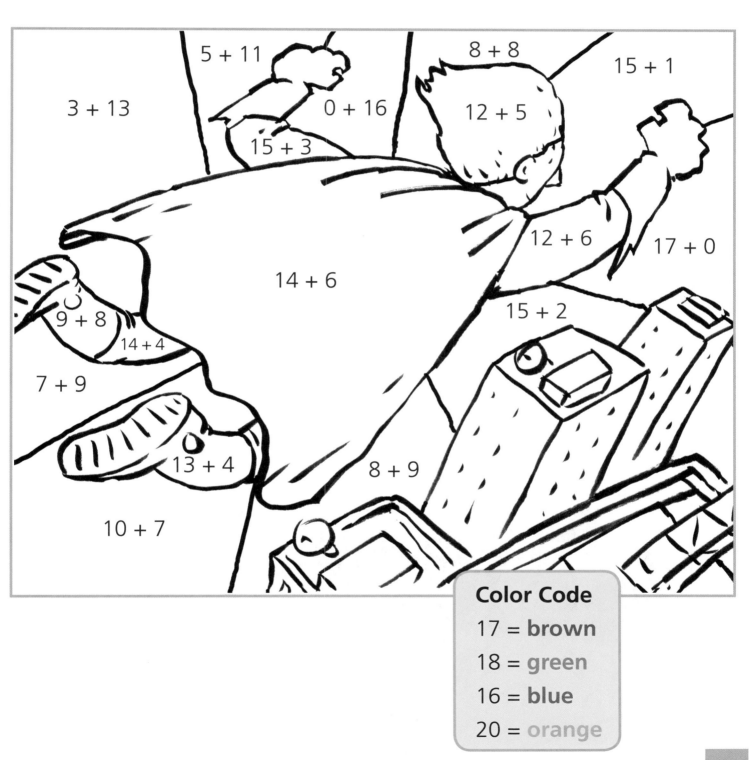

5 + 11

8 + 8

15 + 1

3 + 13

0 + 16

12 + 5

15 + 3

12 + 6

17 + 0

14 + 6

9 + 8

14 + 4

15 + 2

7 + 9

13 + 4

8 + 9

10 + 7

Color Code

17 = **brown**

18 = **green**

16 = **blue**

20 = **orange**

Duck Pond

Quacker, Waddles, Feathers, Billy, and Webby raced to the pond to go swimming. Use the clues in the box below to figure out the order that the ducks got to the water. Then write the names on the lines to show the order.

Quacker is next to Billy.
Waddles is between Billy and Feathers.
Feathers gets to the pond last.
Webby is next to Quacker.

First: _____

_____

_____

_____

Last: _____

Lots of Legs

Solve the problems.

1. A spider has twice as many legs as a dog. There are 3 spiders and 5 dogs. How many legs do the animals have in all?

Legs in all _____

2. A spider has 8 legs. An ant has 6 legs. A tree branch has 3 spiders and 4 ants. How many legs are there of each animal on the tree branch?

Spider legs _____   Ant legs _____

3. There are 3 birds and 4 cats in the yard. How many total legs are on each animal? How many legs in all?

Bird legs _____   Cat legs _____   Legs in all _____

4. There are 5 children, and each one has a cat. How many legs are on the people and the cats altogether?

Legs in all _____

Add It Up

Read the clues. Draw what each person has. Use dollar bills, half dollars, quarters, dimes, nickels, and pennies.

1. Jonah has 2 bills and 3 coins. They add up to $2.16.

2. Margaret has 4 bills and 4 coins. They add up to $5.50.

3. Charlie has 2 bills and 5 coins. They add up to $2.38.

4. Jackie has 2 bills and 2 coins. They add up to $2.30.

5. Wanda has 1 bill and 5 coins. They add up to $1.46.

6. Gus has 3 bills and 3 coins. They add up to $3.07.

How Much Is It?

Solve the problems to find out how much each item costs.
Write the amount in the price tag.

1. The toy cat costs 3 times more than a half dollar.

2. The plate is as much as 6 quarters, 3 dimes, and 2 pennies.

3. The chewing gum costs as much as 4 dimes and 4 nickels.

4. The game costs $1.50 more than 3 dimes and 2 pennies.

5. The swim goggles cost $3.20 more than 2 quarters and 1 dime.

6. The book costs $1.25 more than a half dollar.

Favorite Sports

Look at the bar graph below. Then use it to answer the questions.

Favorite Sports

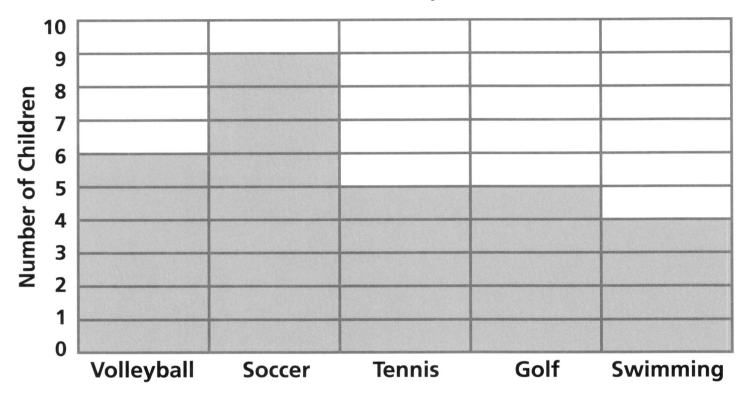

1. How many children were in the survey? _____

2. What is the mode of the data? _____

3. What is the range of the data? _____

4. What is the median of the data? _____

5. How many children like golf and soccer combined? _____

6. Which sport was voted as the favorite? _____

Parts of a Whole

Look at each shape. Write the fraction that describes the amount each shape is colored.

1.

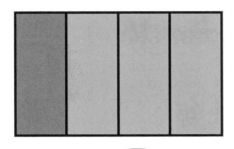

Green:

Orange: ⬭

2.

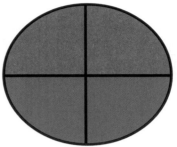

Blue:

Red: ⬭

3.

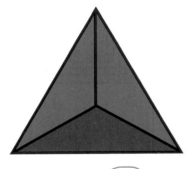

Purple:

Red: ⬭

4.

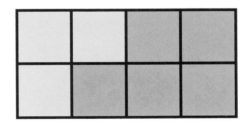

Yellow:

Orange: ⬭

Squares Everywhere!

Gloria must find **all** of the squares in each picture.
Help her by writing the number of squares on the line.

1.

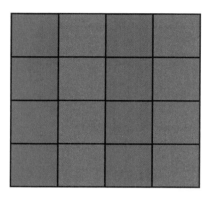

_____ squares

2.

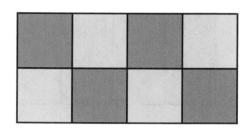

_____ squares

3.

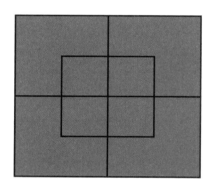

_____ squares

4.

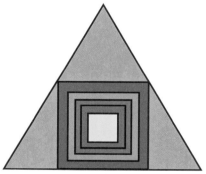

_____ squares

5.

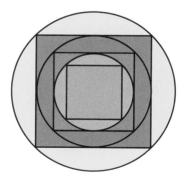

_____ squares

6.

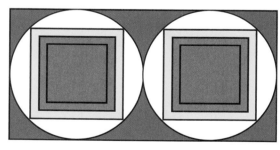

_____ squares

Homework Days

The line graph below shows the number of students who finished their homework each day last week. Read the graph and answer the questions.

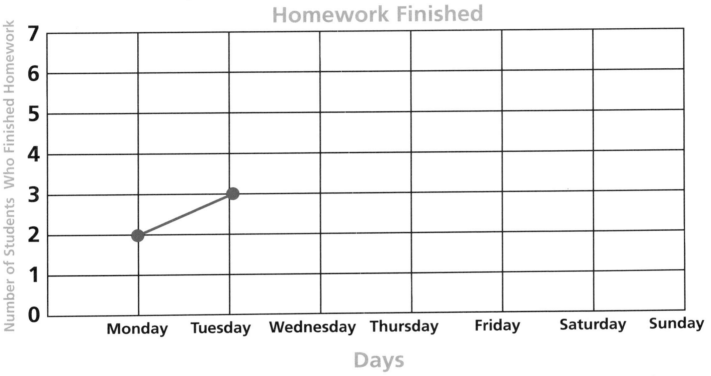

Homework Finished

Days

1. On Wednesday, 6 students finished their homework. Plot the data on the graph.

2. On Thursday, 4 students finished their homework. Plot the data on the graph.

3. On Friday, 3 students finished their homework. Plot the data on the graph.

4. On which day did most students finish their homework?

   _____

5. How many more students finished their homework on Wednesday than on Monday?

   _____

Making Dinner

Mrs. Morgan makes dinner for three nights. She makes spaghetti, hamburgers, and chicken. Use the clues in the box below to find out which dinner she will serve on which night. Fill in the chart to help you.

> Spaghetti will not be served on Friday.
> Hamburgers will not be served on Saturday.
> Chicken will not be served on Sunday.
> The dinner that will be served on Friday has the most letters in its name.

	Spaghetti	Hamburgers	Chicken
Friday			
Saturday			
Sunday			

1. On Friday, Mrs. Morgan will serve _____.

2. On Saturday, Mrs. Morgan will serve _____.

3. On Sunday, Mrs. Morgan will serve _____.

Take Your Time

Draw a line from each activity to the amount of time it takes to do it.

1.

adding two numbers

2.

eating a sandwich

hours

3.

drawing and coloring a house

minutes

4.

watching a movie

seconds

5.

enjoying a birthday party

Giraffe Lineup

There are four giraffes at the zoo. Solve the problems below to find out how tall each giraffe is.

Sammy **Sally** **Stretch** **Super Stretch**

1. Sammy is the height of three yardsticks. How many feet tall is Sammy? _____

2. Stretch is twice the height of Sammy, minus 5 feet. How tall is Stretch? _____

3. Sally is two feet shorter than Stretch. How tall is Sally? _____

4. Super Stretch is 5 feet taller than Sally. How tall is Super Stretch? _____

How Much?

Read the clues. Draw what each person has. Use dollar bills, half dollars, quarters, dimes, nickels, and pennies.

1. Kim has 2 bills and 4 coins. They add up to $2.37.

2. Saj has 2 bills and 4 coins. They add up to $3.00.

3. Caleb has 3 bills and 3 coins. They add up to $3.76.

4. Arthur has 2 bills and 3 coins. They add up to $3.25.

5. Janie has 2 bills and 5 coins. They add up to $2.33.

6. Yvonne has 1 bill and 6 coins. They add up to $2.20.

What's the Order?

Each group of numbers below can be made into three-digit numbers. Rearrange the digits to write the smallest and the largest three-digit numbers possible. Write the numbers on the lines.

1.

smallest
number _____

largest
number _____

2.

smallest
number _____

largest
number _____

3.

smallest
number _____

largest
number _____

4.

smallest
number _____

largest
number _____

5.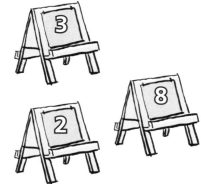

smallest
number _____

largest
number _____

6.

smallest
number _____

largest
number _____

What Number Am I Thinking Of?

Solve the riddles below. Use the numbers 0 to 9 to write the correct two-digit number on each crystal ball.

1. The sum of the digits is 5. Their difference is 3. The number is odd.

2. The sum of the digits is 10. Their difference is 6. The number is even.

3. The sum of the digits is 14. Their difference is 0. The number is odd.

4. The sum of the digits is 8. Their difference is 4. The number is even.

5. The sum of the digits is 8. Their difference is 2. The number is odd.

6. The sum of the digits is 9. Their difference is 9. The number is even.

The Bike Store

Solve the problems.

1. Julia's bike had to be fixed 4 times in one year. If her bike continues to break at the same rate, how many times will the bike have to be fixed in 6 years?

_____

2. Mr. Marshall can fix 5 bicycles each day. The store is closed on the weekends. How many days would it take Mr. Marshall to fix 15 bikes?

_____

3. Each bicycle in Mr. Marshall's shop has 2 wheels. How many bikes are in the shop if there are 120 wheels?

_____

4. There are 250 bicycles in the bike shop. How many total wheels are on these bikes in the shop?

_____

Fill in the Blanks!

Write **+** or **–** in the circles to make the number sentences true.
The number sentences should be read from left to right.

1. $15 \bigcirc 3 \bigcirc 6 = 18$

2. $7 \bigcirc 4 \bigcirc 4 = 15$

3. $16 \bigcirc 7 \bigcirc 6 = 3$

4. $17 \bigcirc 4 \bigcirc 8 = 13$

5. $8 \bigcirc 9 \bigcirc 5 = 12$

6. $9 \bigcirc 3 \bigcirc 6 = 18$

7. $22 \bigcirc 11 \bigcirc 4 = 7$

8. $15 \bigcirc 6 \bigcirc 5 = 16$

What Comes Next?

Look at the pattern in each row. Draw the shape that should come next.

1. _____

2. _____

3. _____

4. _____

5. _____

Zoo Patterns

Figure out each pattern below. Then write the rule and finish the pattern.

1.

What is the rule of the pattern?

_____

2.

What is the rule of the pattern?

_____

3.

What is the rule of the pattern?

_____

4.

What is the rule of the pattern?

_____

5.

What is the rule of the pattern?

_____

Max's Two Fish

Max looks at the fish at the pet store. The store has orange, brown, yellow, and blue fish. Max can buy only two fish. Color each pair of fish below to show how many combinations of colors he can buy.

Pick a Crayon

Franny will pick a crayon from the jar. Which crayon color do you think Franny will pick? Look at each jar of crayons. Write the name of the colors she is most and least likely to pick.

		Most Likely	Least Likely
1.			
2.			
3.			
4.			

Circle Time

Color each circle to show the correct fraction.

1. Color $\frac{3}{7}$ purple. Color $\frac{4}{7}$ yellow.

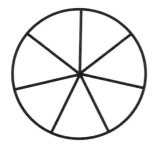

2. Color $\frac{3}{6}$ green. Color $\frac{2}{6}$ red. Color $\frac{1}{6}$ blue.

3. Color $\frac{1}{4}$ orange. Color $\frac{3}{4}$ red.

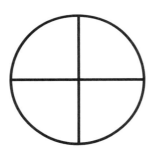

4. Color $\frac{1}{3}$ purple. Color $\frac{2}{3}$ yellow.

5. Color $\frac{3}{5}$ blue. Color $\frac{2}{5}$ orange.

6. Color $\frac{4}{8}$ green. Color $\frac{3}{8}$ red. Color $\frac{1}{8}$ blue.

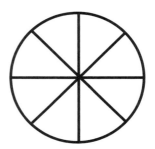

Pizza Fractions

Jay had a pizza at his birthday party. The pizza was cut into 12 equal pieces. Solve the problems about the pizza.

1. What fraction of the pizza describes one slice? _____

2. What fraction of the pizza describes 2 slices? _____

3. Jay and his best friend eat 5 slices in all. What fraction of the pizza is 5 slices? _____

4. How many slices make up one-half of the pizza? _____

5. How many slices make up one-fourth of the pizza? _____

6. How many slices make up one-third of the pizza? _____

Where Are the Triangles?

Sam must find **all** of the triangles in each picture.
Help him by writing the number of triangles on the line.

1.

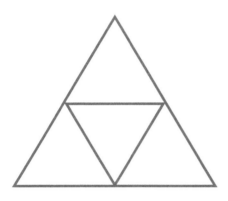

_____ triangles

2.

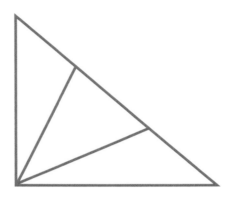

_____ triangles

3.

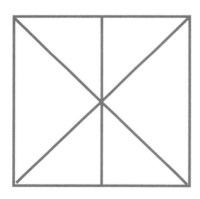

_____ triangles

4.

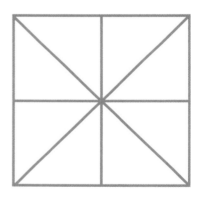

_____ triangles

5.

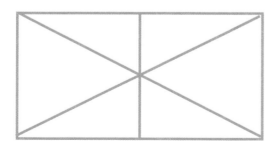

_____ triangles

6.

_____ triangles

Exploring Figures

Circle the figure that has the correct number of faces, edges, and vertices.

1. 6 faces, 12 edges, 8 vertices

2. 0 faces, 0 edges, 0 vertices

3. 1 face, 0 edges, 1 vertex

4. 5 faces, 9 edges, 6 vertices

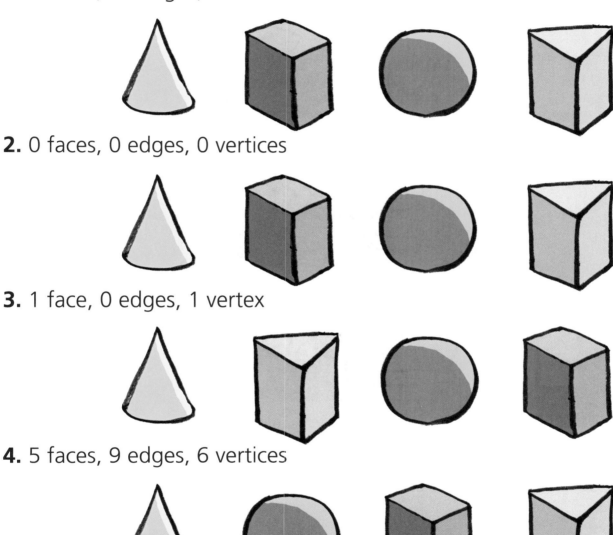

5. How is a cube like a rectangle? Write a sentence to explain it.

_____

_____

Numbers Big and Small

Help the monkey make four-digit numbers from its four numbers. Make as many four-digit numbers as you can on the lines below.

_____ _____ _____ _____

_____ _____ _____ _____

_____ _____ _____ _____

_____ _____ _____ _____

Room Numbers

Help Jacob find the two-digit room numbers he is looking for. Use the digits 1–9 to write the two-digit numbers that belong on each hotel room door.

1. The sum of the digits is 10. Their difference is 4. The number is odd.

2. The sum of the digits is 8. Their difference is 4. The number is even.

3. The sum of the digits is 16. Their difference is 0. The number is even.

4. The sum of the digits is 6. Their difference is 2. The number is even.

5. The sum of the digits is 3. Their difference is 1. The number is odd.

6. The sum of the digits is 11. Their difference is 1. The number is odd.

What Number Am I?

Solve the riddles below. Then write the number on the line.

1. I am a two-digit even number.
The sum of my numbers is 13.
The difference of my numbers
is 1.
I am between 50 and 100.

What number am I? _____

2. I am a three-digit number.
The numbers in my ones, tens,
and hundreds places are all
the same.
The sum of my numbers is 9.

What number am I? _____

3. I am a two-digit number.
The numbers in my ones place is
half the number in my tens
place.
The sum of my numbers is 6.

What number am I? _____

4. I am a three-digit number.
The sum of my numbers is 16.
My hundreds digit is 7.
My ones digit is 4.

What number am I? _____

What's the Rule?

Figure out each pattern below. Then write the rule and finish the pattern.

1.

| 38 | 42 | 46 | 50 | | | | |

What is the rule of the pattern?_____

2. (721) (719) (717) (715) ( ) ( ) ( ) ( )

What is the rule of the pattern?_____

3. 75 70 65 60 △ △ △ △

What is the rule of the pattern?_____

4. 30 45 60 75

What is the rule of the pattern?_____

5. 120 220 320 420

What is the rule of the pattern?_____

6. Write your own pattern.

What is the rule of the pattern?_____

Harry's Camp Clothes

Harry packed clothes for summer camp. He packed a blue shirt, a green shirt, and a red shirt. He packed blue pants, black pants, and brown pants. Color the pictures to show how many different combinations of shirts and pants Harry can wear.

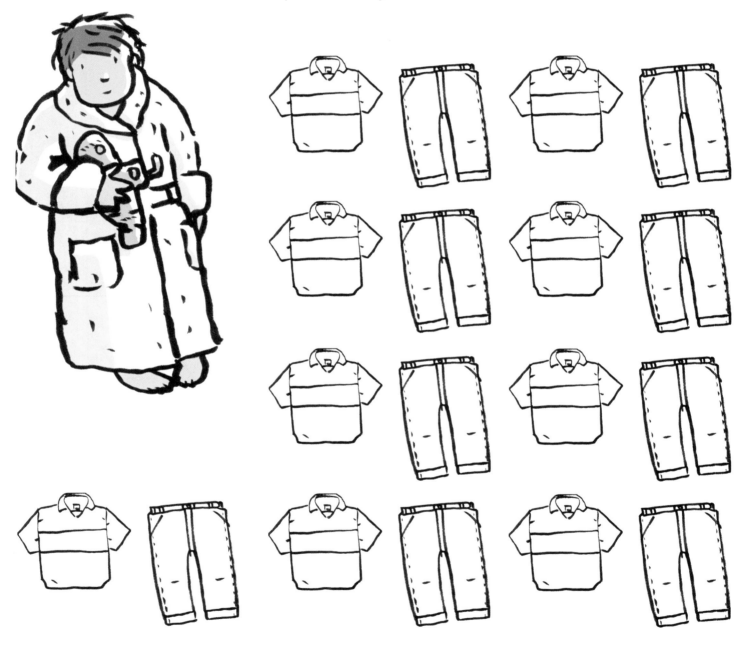

Count Them Up!

Write the number of faces, edges, and vertices for each shape shown.

1.

_____ faces

_____ edges

_____ vertices

2.

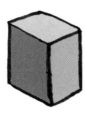

_____ faces

_____ edges

_____ vertices

3.

_____ faces

_____ edges

_____ vertices

4.

_____ faces

_____ edges

_____ vertices

5.

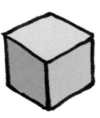

_____ faces

_____ edges

_____ vertices

6.

_____ faces

_____ edges

_____ vertices

Shape Riddles

Solve each riddle and write the name of the robot on the line.

1. My head is made of 4 sides and my body has no edges. Who am I?

_____

2. My feet are the same shape as my ears. Who am I?

_____

3. I have a different number of sides on each arm. Who am I?

_____

4. My arms and legs have no edges. Who am I?

_____

5. Draw a robot that looks
like Rita but has Henry's head.

Turn Those Shapes!

Look at the shapes in each row. Circle the shape that does not belong.

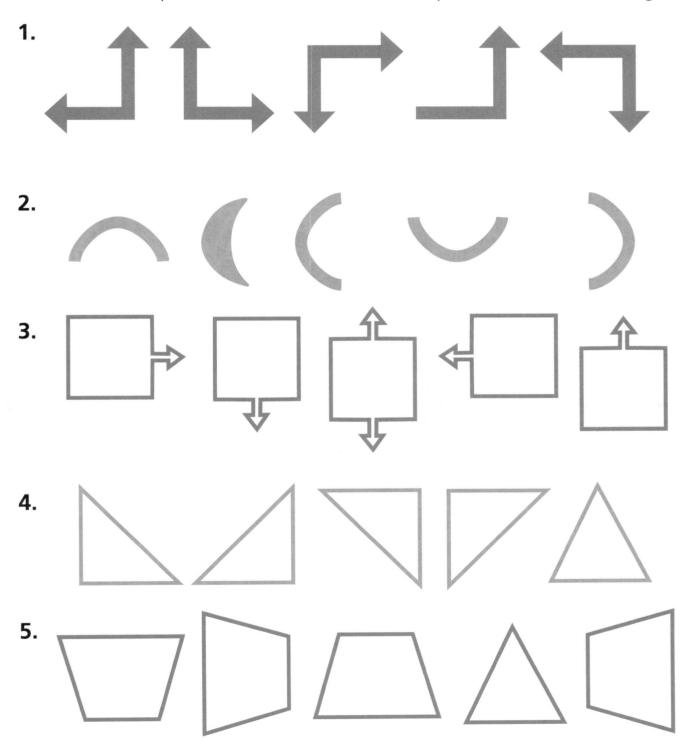

1.

2.

3.

4.

5.

Cake for Everyone!

Mrs. Marcos baked a cake for her class.
She divided the cake into 16 equal slices.
There are 16 children in her class.
Solve the problems below about the cake.

1. Each student gets one slice of cake. What fraction of the cake would 3 students eat? _____

2. How many slices of cake make up $\frac{1}{2}$ of the cake? _____

3. How many slices of cake make up $\frac{1}{4}$ of the cake? _____

4. What fraction shows how much of the cake 7 students will eat? _____

5. What fraction shows one slice of the cake? _____

6. What fraction shows 10 slices of the cake? _____

Divide and Conquer!

Solve the problems.

1. There are 20 students in Melissa's class. They split into 4 equal teams to play games. How many students are on each team?

   _____

2. What fraction describes one student on Melissa's team? _____

3. What fraction describes two whole teams together? _____

4. How many students are on two teams? _____

5. It takes two students on each team to carry the sports equipment. What fraction describes the number of students on a team that carry the equipment? _____

6. One student on each team is absent today. What fraction describes how much of the whole class is absent today? _____

Fun Run

Jen's class had a fun run. The first five people to cross the finish line were Jen, Amrita, Katie, Ashley, and Alicia. Use the clues in the box below to find out in what order the girls finished the race. Then write their names under their pictures.

> Ashley is next to Jen.
>
> Jen is next to Katie.
>
> Ashley is at the front.
>
> Amrita is between Alicia and Katie.

_____ _____ _____ _____ _____

Hidden Subtraction

Find the answer to each number sentence. Use each answer and the code below to color the spaces. Find the hidden picture.

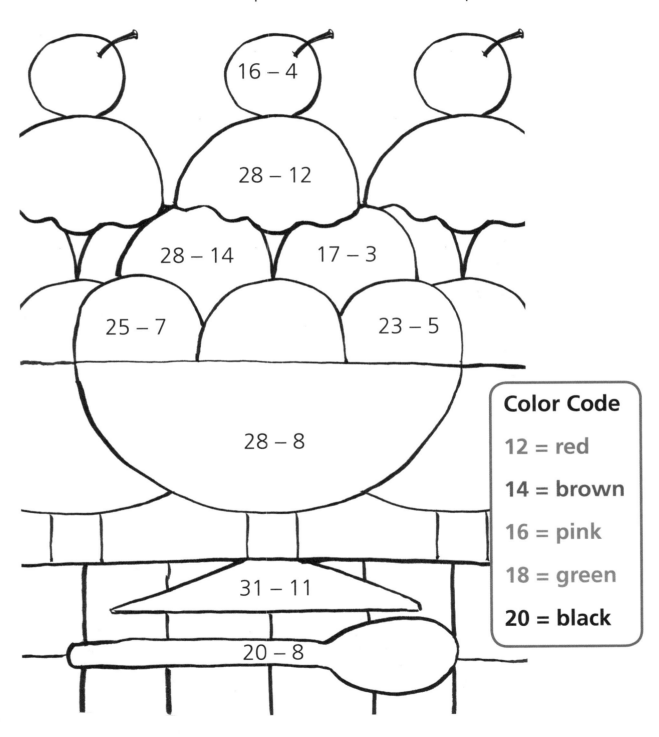

16 – 4

28 – 12

28 – 14   17 – 3

25 – 7   23 – 5

28 – 8

31 – 11

20 – 8

Color Code

12 = red

14 = brown

16 = pink

18 = green

20 = black

Missing Questions

The questions are missing from the problems below. Read each problem and each answer. Then write a question that makes sense in the problem.

1. Jeff has 14 baseball cards. Tony has 23 baseball cards.

Question: _____

_____

Answer: 37 baseball cards

2. Joni has 3 quarters. Her sister has 4 quarters.

Question: _____

_____

Answer: $1.75

3. Darren swims 10 laps in the pool each day.

Question: _____

_____

Answer: 50

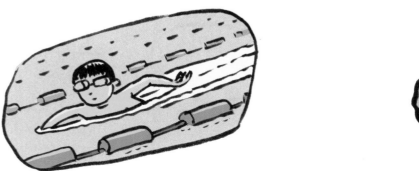

4. Mom made 14 pies. She sent 10 pies to the bake sale.

Question: _____

_____

Answer: 4

Compare Time

Read what each pair of children is saying. Then answer the question.

1.

Roy: I will be finished with my homework in 55 minutes.

Sara: I will be finished with my homework in 1 hour.

Who will finish his or her homework first? _____

2.

Donna: I will be on vacation for 1 week.

Mary: I will be on vacation for 9 days.

Who will be on vacation longest? _____

3.

Javier: It took me 2 minutes to brush my teeth.

Isabella: It took me 95 seconds to brush my teeth.

Who took a longer time to brush his or her teeth?

_____

4.

Raul: I finished this book 3 weeks ago.

Rico: I finished this book 1 month ago.

Who finished the book first?

_____

Class Schedule

Read the list of things Jack's class must do today.
Use the list to answer the questions.

9:00 circle time

9:15 center time

9:45 math

10:30 reading

11:30 lunch

12:00 gym hour

1. How long does Jack's class have center time? _____

2. Which activity takes longer, math or reading? _____

3. How long before gym does lunchtime start? _____

4. How long does Jack's class spend in math each day?

_____

5. What is the shortest activity of the day? _____

6. What will Jack's classmates be doing at 11:00? _____

Inches or Feet?

Write **inches** or **feet** to complete each sentence below.
Choose the unit of length that makes the most sense.

1. George's room is 15 _____ long.

2. Mom's flowers are about 11 _____ long.

3. Natalia's computer is 1 _____ long.

4. Ted's boot is 10 _____ long.

5. Becky's shirt is 16 _____ long.

6. Dad's shovel is 4 _____ long.

7. Maurice's pencil is 7 _____ long.

8. Ms. Carmin's car is 10 _____ long.

Favorite Movie

Look at the bar graph below. Then answer the questions.

Favorite Movie

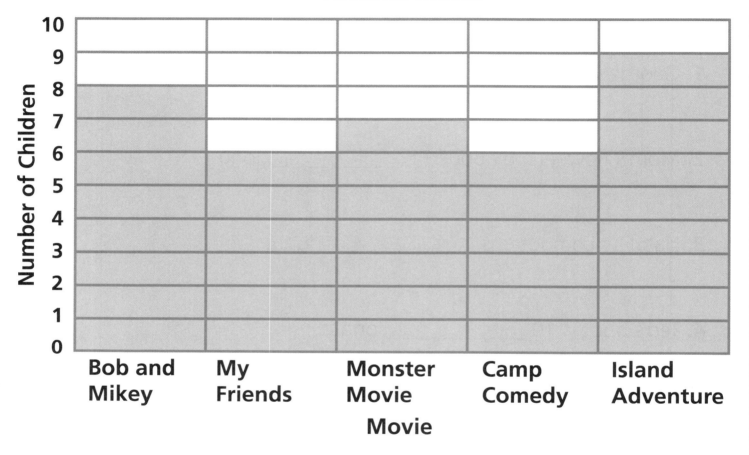

1. How many children voted for **Camp Comedy** as their favorite movie? _____

2. What is the total number of people who voted for their favorite movie? _____

3. Which movie received 7 votes? _____

4. What is the range of the data? _____

5. What is the mode of the data? _____

6. What is the median of the data? _____

Take a Turn

Look at each shape in column 1. Draw a line to the picture in column 2 that shows the shape turned once to the left.

Column 1   **Column 2**

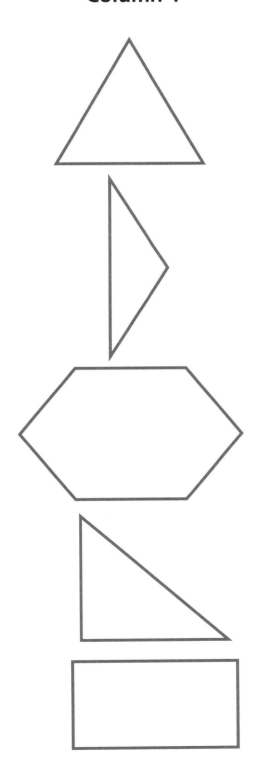
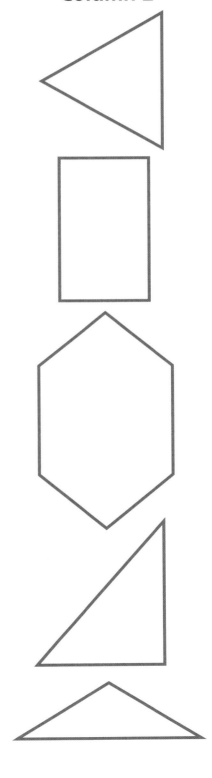

Whose Shapes?

Look at the clues to find out who drew each picture. Then write the name of each child beneath his or her drawing.

Jenna: My picture has shapes with no vertices.

Carmen: My picture shows one shape divided into 6 smaller ones.

Tony: My picture is made of 4 triangles.

Manuel: My picture has 10 vertices.

Jennifer: My picture has 7 vertices.

Aaron: My picture shows 4 overlapping figures.

1.

_____

2.

_____

3.

_____

4.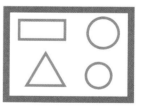

_____

5.

_____

6.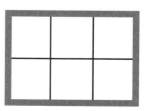

_____

Shape Riddles

Look at the shapes below to solve the riddles. Write the letter that answers each riddle on the line.

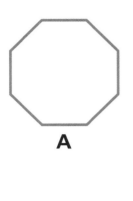

A

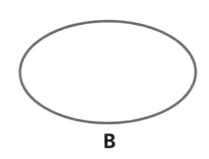

B

C

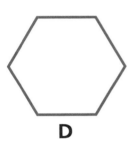

D

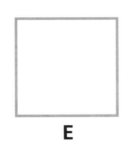

E

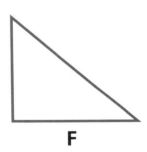

F

1. You can fit 5 triangles in my outline. Who am I? _____

2. You can turn me into two rectangles. Who am I? _____

3. You can use two of me to make a square. Who am I?

_____

4. I have the same number of sides as two rectangles. Who am I?

_____

5. I have two more sides than a square. Who am I? _____

6. I have two fewer sides than a triangle. Who am I?

_____

Car Patterns

Look at the pattern of numbers. Then complete the pattern.

1. 333 336 339

2. 412 424 436

3. 207 307 407

4. 999 996 993

5. 755 750 745

6. 826 830 834

Which Is Bigger?

Circle the figure that shows the larger fraction colored.

1.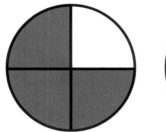

2.

3.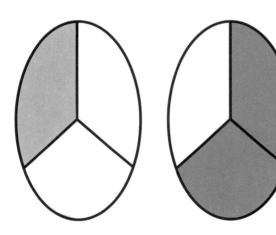

4.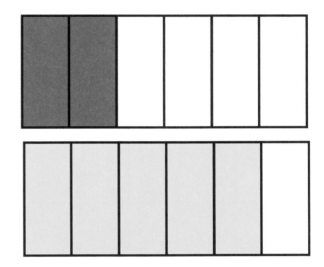

5.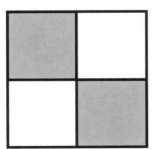

6.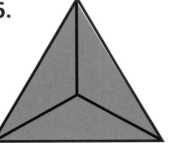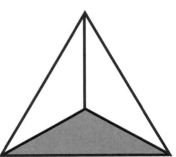

Dog Walker

Sally is a dog walker. She walks only three dogs at a time. Write the different combinations of dogs that Sally can walk at once.

Fido   **Lou**   **Fluffy**   **Spike**

_____ _____ _____

_____ _____ _____

_____ _____ _____

_____ _____ _____

Pick a Coin

Raphael will pick a coin from the jar. Which coin do you think Raphael will pick? Look at each jar of coins. Write the name of the coin in each box to show which coin he is most or least likely to pick.

	Most Likely	Least Likely
1.		
2.		
3.		
4.		

Dog Parade

Patsy, Sadie, Mr. Wiggles, Rex, and Foxy are in a dog parade. Use the clues in the box below to write the names of the dogs in the correct order.

Patsy is walking in front of Sadie.

Foxy is walking between Mr. Wiggles and Patsy.

Mr. Wiggles is walking behind Rex.

Rex is the leader.

_____ _____ _____ _____ _____
First   **Last**

What Is the Question?

The questions are missing from the problems below. Read each problem and each answer. Then write a question that makes sense in the problem.

1. A math test has 24 questions. Debbie answers 13 questions.

Question: _____

Answer: 11

2. A book has 14 chapters. Gerard just finished reading Chapter 5.

Question: _____

Answer: 9

3. Mom has 5 grocery bags. Each bag has 10 items in it.

Question: _____

Answer: 50

4. Irving brushes his teeth three times each day.

Question: _____

Answer: 12

Copy That Picture!

Help the hippo make another drawing just like the first one. Draw each picture you see. Try not to go over any line twice, and try not to lift your pencil. Can you do it?

1.

2.

3.

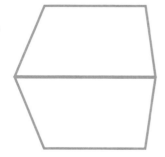

4.

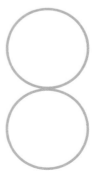

Which Takes Longer?

Circle the event that takes a longer amount of time to do.

1.

saying your name   combing your hair

2.

making a pizza   singing a song

3.

making your bed   playing a soccer game

4.

eating a sandwich   reading a book

5.

riding in an airplane   riding your bike

How Long Is It?

Solve the problems.

1. Helene's swing set is 76 feet from the back door of her house. If she runs 32 feet to the swing set and then walks the rest of the way, how many feet will Helene walk to the swing set? _____

2. Mr. Lee's class is building a birdhouse. They need 4 pieces of wood that are each 6 inches long. How many inches of wood will they need for their birdhouse in all? _____

3. Maggie skips 43 feet from the school cafeteria to her classroom. How many total feet would Maggie have to skip if she went from the cafeteria to the classroom and then back again? _____

4. Julian's bedroom wall is 15 feet long. He wants to put up a picture frame that is 24 inches long. How many feet on Julian's wall will the picture frame take up? _____

Match the Coins

Draw a line between groups of money that have the same value.

Who Am I?

All of these children are different ages. Solve the riddles below.

Maria   Danny   Gabrielle   Millie   Harry   Pete

1. I am a boy who is younger than Pete. Who am I?

_____

2. I am older than Danny but younger than Gabrielle. Who am I?

_____

3. I am a girl who is older than Gabrielle. Who am I?

_____

4. I am older than the oldest girl. Who am I? _____

5. I am two years older than Millie. Who am I?

_____

6. I am three years younger than the oldest child. Who am I?

_____

Number Riddles

The train cars below are out of order.
Solve the riddles to put the trains in the correct order.

1. The number is even. It is greater than 400. It is less than 500. _____

2. The number is odd. It is greater than 1,000. It is less than 1,100.

_____

3. The number is even. It is greater than 600 and less than 700. _____

4. The number is odd. It is greater than 860 and less than 890. _____

5. The number is odd. It is greater than 480 and less than 550. _____

6. The number is even. It is greater than 4,000 and less than 4,500.

_____

Bug Patterns

Figure out each pattern below. Then finish the pattern.

1.

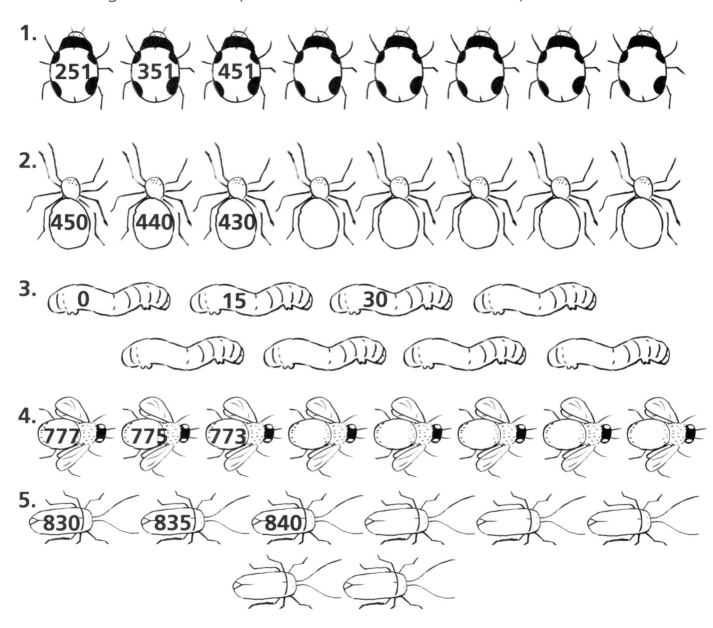

251 351 451

2. 450 440 430

3. 0 15 30

4. 777 775 773

5. 830 835 840

6. Write your own number pattern below.

____ ____ ____ ____ ____

Letters Everywhere!

Figure out each pattern below. Then finish the pattern.

1. W, W, A, W, W, B, W, W, C,

_____, _____, _____, _____, _____, _____, _____, _____

2. A, C, C, D, F, F, G, I, I,

_____, _____, _____, _____, _____, _____, _____, _____

3. Z, Y, X, W, V, U, T, S,

_____, _____, _____, _____, _____, _____, _____, _____

4. A, B, B, C, C, C, D, D, D, D,

_____, _____, _____, _____, _____, _____, _____, _____

5. G, H, I, I, J, K, L, L, M, N,

_____, _____, _____, _____, _____, _____, _____, _____

Snack Time!

Read the clues to find out how much each item costs.
Write the amount in the price tag.

1. The candy costs $2.00 more than a quarter, dime, nickel, and penny.

2. The popcorn costs $1.30 more than 2 dimes and 4 pennies.

3. The pretzels cost 50 cents more than 3 dimes, 1 nickel, and 3 pennies.

4. The granola bar costs 50 cents more than a quarter, 2 dimes, and a nickel.

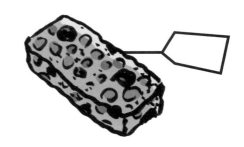

5. The cookies cost 30 cents more than a dime and 3 pennies.

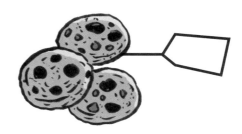

Look at the Menu

Look at the prices of the foods on the list.
Use the prices to solve the problems.

hot dog	$2.40
hamburger	$3.00
spaghetti	$2.50
grilled cheese	$2.10

1. Mona bought two food items that were the same. She spent $5.00. What food did she buy? _____

2. Alec bought a grilled cheese and a hot dog. How much did he spend in all? _____

3. How much would Donny spend if he bought a hamburger along with a drink that costs 75 cents? _____

4. Jen bought 2 grilled cheese sandwiches. How much did she spend in all? _____

Favorite Colors

Students in Evan's class voted on their favorite colors. Evan made a tally chart of the votes. Use the tally chart to help you complete the bar graph of the class votes.

Favorite Colors

Color	Tally
green	卌
purple	II
blue	IIII
orange	卌
red	III

Number of Votes

Colors

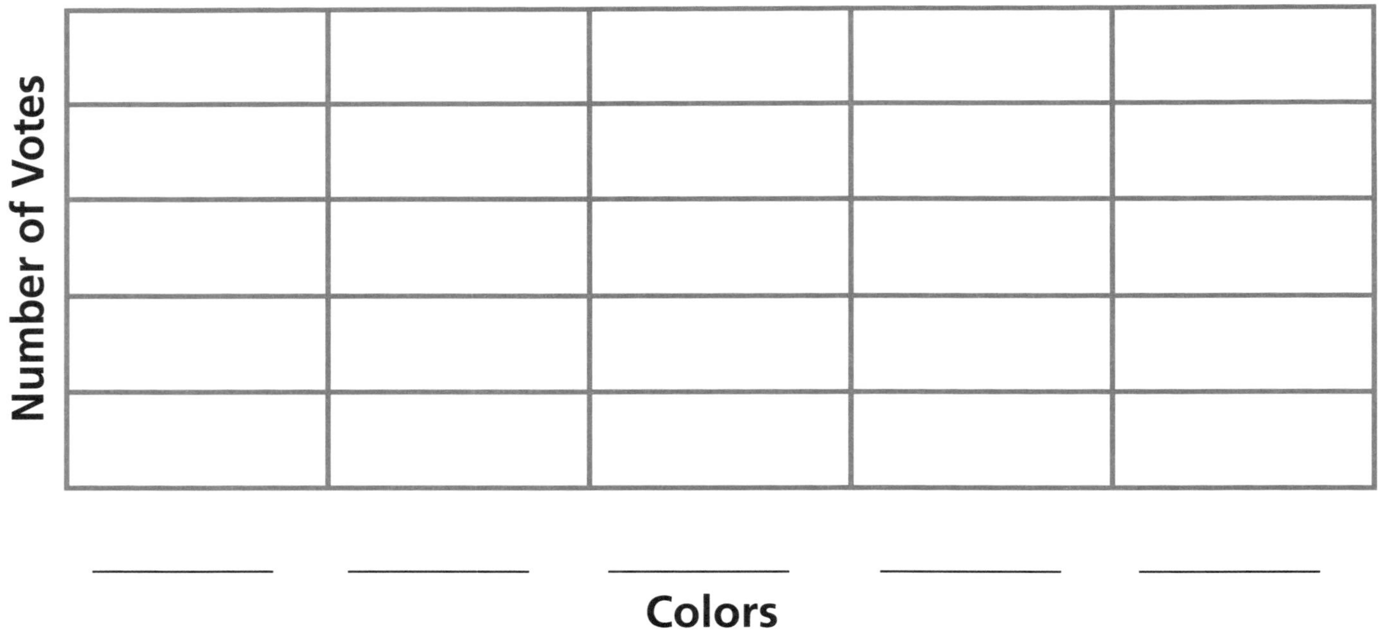

How many children voted for their favorite color? _____

Make a Bar Graph

Lily's Music Center started classes this week. There will be 7 students in the guitar class. There will be 8 kids in the drums class. There will be 5 kids in the piano class, and 4 kids in the trumpet class.

Use the information above to help you complete the bar graph about music classes.

Number of Students

Classes

Beach Fun

Solve the problems.

1. There are 36 people at the beach at 11:00. During the next hour, 23 more people arrive. How many people are at the beach at 12:00? _____

2. Jason collected 24 seashells. His mother collected 14 seashells. How many more will Jason and his mom need in order to collect 50 seashells? _____

3. Grey and Mandy each went jogging on the beach for 3 days in a row. Grey jogged 3 miles each day. Mandy jogged 6 miles each day. How many miles did they jog in all? _____

4. Sarah used 34 buckets of sand to make her sand castle. When a wave destroyed it she made another one exactly like the first. How many buckets of sand did Sarah use in all? _____

Timing the Tides

Ocean tides come in every six hours and go back out every six hours. Use this information to solve the problems below.

1. The tide is in at 3:00 in the afternoon. Will the tide be in or out at 9:00 the next morning?

_____

2. The tide is out at 8:30 in the morning. At what time will the tide be halfway in?

_____

3. Abby went to the beach at 10:00 in the morning. The tide was all the way in when she arrived. She left when the tide was all the way out. What time did Abby leave the beach?

_____

4. The tide is out at 9:30 at night. Will the tide be in or out at 3:30 the next afternoon?

_____

Groups of Shapes

Circle the shapes that belong in each group.

1. shapes with more than 3 sides

2. shapes with more than 3 vertices

3. shapes with no right angles

4. shapes with more than 4 sides

5. Write a title to describe this group of shapes.

Animal Shapes

Solve the riddles below. Write the name of the animal that each riddle describes.

horse

rabbit

giraffe

dog

1. My ears and tail are the same shape. What am I?

_____

2. I am made of shapes with no vertices. What am I?

_____

3. All of my shapes are made of right angles. What am I?

_____

4. Only one shape on my body has no corners. What am I?

_____

Which Is Smaller?

Circle the shape that shows the smaller fraction colored.

1.

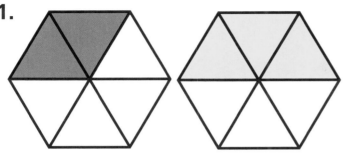

2.

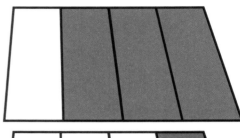

3.

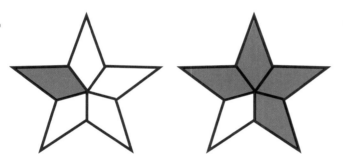

4.

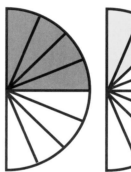

5.

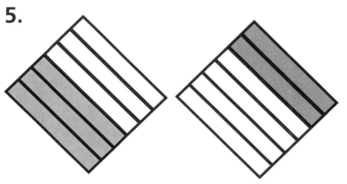

6.

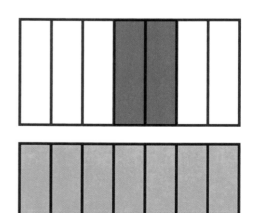

Fraction Problems

Solve the problems.

1. Penelope ate $\frac{1}{2}$ of her banana. Then her mom ate $\frac{1}{2}$ of the banana. Write a fraction to show how much of the banana was eaten.

_____

2. Jessie read $\frac{1}{3}$ of his book on Monday. He read $\frac{1}{3}$ of the book on Tuesday. How much of the book did he read in all?

_____

3. Mom baked an apple pie and brought $\frac{1}{4}$ of it to grandma's house. How much of the pie did Mom leave at home?

_____

4. Mom saw the first $\frac{1}{4}$ of the baseball game. Dad saw the second $\frac{1}{4}$ of the baseball game. How much of the whole game did Mom and Dad see altogether?

_____

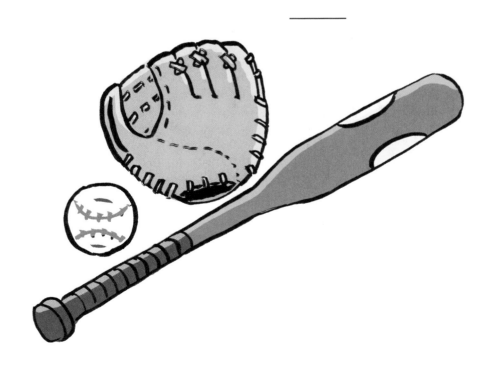

School Days

Solve the problems.

1. There are 12 days before the end of school. Four of those days are weekends. How many weekdays are left before the end of school? _____

2. Kayla has been in school for 56 days. She has had gym class 22 times so far. How many days did Kayla have school without going to gym class? _____

3. Roger had spring break 18 days ago. Today it is the 29th. When did spring break begin? _____

4. There are 25 days left of summer break. Beatrice and her family will be on vacation for 12 of those days. How many days are left of summer that Beatrice will not be on vacation? _____

Fill in the Missing Signs

Write **+** or **−** in the circles to make the number sentences true.
The number sentences should be read from left to right.

1. 12 ◯ 8 ◯ 5 = 15

2. 9 ◯ 4 ◯ 7 = 20

3. 8 ◯ 6 ◯ 2 = 0

4. 7 ◯ 3 ◯ 14 = 18

5. 5 ◯ 12 ◯ 3 = 14

6. 7 ◯ 3 ◯ 8 = 18

7. 15 ◯ 6 ◯ 4 = 13

8. 16 ◯ 7 ◯ 8 = 1

Subtraction Puzzles

Look at each set of numbers on the tulips. Use the numbers to fill in the blanks in the number problems. Use each number only once in a problem.

1.

$$\begin{array}{r} \square\,6 \\ -\ 7\,\square \\ \hline \square\,1 \end{array} \qquad \begin{array}{r} \square\ \square \\ -\ 1\ \square \\ \hline 1\quad 4 \end{array}$$

2.

$$\begin{array}{r} \square\,0 \\ -\ 1\,\square \\ \hline \square\,0 \end{array} \qquad \begin{array}{r} \square\ \square \\ -\ 2\ \square \\ \hline 3\quad 4 \end{array}$$

3.

$$\begin{array}{r} \square\,7 \\ -\ \square\,5 \\ \hline \square\,2 \end{array} \qquad \begin{array}{r} 4\ \square \\ -\ \square\ 2 \\ \hline 2\ \square \end{array}$$

4.

$$\begin{array}{r} \square\,8 \\ -\ 3\,\square \\ \hline 3\,\square \end{array} \qquad \begin{array}{r} \square\ \square \\ -\ 3\ 4 \\ \hline 3\ \square \end{array}$$

Find the Mystery Numbers

Use the clues to write the mystery numbers.

1. I am an even number that is more than 5,502 and less than 5,510. I could be

_____, _____, or _____.

2. I am an even number that is between 25 and 40 and can be divided by 5. I can only be _____.

3. I am less than 900. The number in my ones place is 2. The number in my tens place is double the number in my ones place. The number in my hundreds place is double the number in my tens place. I am _____.

4. I am an even number between 70 and 100. The number in my tens place is double the number in my ones place. I am _____.

5. I am less than 30. The number in my tens place is double the number in my ones place. I can only be _____.

Write It Again and Again

Answer each question by writing the number and the word.

1. What number has 3 thousands, 4 hundreds, 7 tens, and 8 ones?

Write the number. _____ Write the word. _____

_____

2. What number has 8 hundreds, 3 tens, and 0 ones?

Write the number. _____ Write the word. _____

_____

3. What number has 0 thousands, 4 hundreds, 0 tens, and 0 ones?

Write the number. _____ Write the word. _____

_____

4. What number has 5 hundreds, 2 tens, and 9 ones?

Write the number. _____ Write the word. _____

_____

5. What number has 7 thousands, 8 hundreds, 3 tens, and 4 ones?

Write the number. _____ Write the word. _____

_____

6. What number has 4 thousands, 0 hundreds, 5 tens, and 2 ones?

Write the number. _____ Write the word. _____

_____

Brooke the Ballerina

Brooke wears pink and white to dance class. She has a leotard, tights, and a skirt in white. She also has a leotard, tights, and a skirt in pink. Color the pictures to show how many different ways Brooke can combine her clothes for dance class.

What's Missing?

Look at each set of numbers on the shirts. Use the numbers to fill in the blanks in the number problems. Use each number only once in a problem.

1.

```
  □   3              1   □
+ 1   □            + 7   6
―――――――            ―――――――
  □   4            □   □
```

2.

```
  □   6              □   7
  □   □            - 2   □
―――――――            ―――――――
  2   4              □   5
```

3.

```
  □   5              6   □
- 2   □            - □   5
―――――――            ―――――――
  3   □              7   □
```

4.

```
  □   3              6   □
- 5   2            - □   □
―――――――            ―――――――
  □   □              5   5
```

At the Dump

Solve the problems.

1. The garbage truck picks up trash from 72 houses. There are 51 houses that also have recycling to be picked up. How many of the houses do not have any recycling to be picked up? _____

2. A garbage truck stops at 46 houses with even-numbered addresses. Every other one of these houses has 2 cans of garbage. How many houses with even-numbered addresses have 2 cans of garbage to put out? _____

3. The garbage can at Mr. King's house has 27 bags in it. Mr. Mazza's trash can has 14 bags in it. How many more bags does Mr. King have in his garbage can than Mr. Mazza? _____

4. The garbage truck can hold 245 bags of trash. How many more bags can it fit if it already has 114 bags in it? _____

Squirrels at the Bird Feeder

Use the information below to make a line graph.

Claudia made a bird feeder. Sometimes squirrels also visit the feeder. On Monday, 3 squirrels visited the feeder. On Tuesday and Wednesday, 4 squirrels visited. On Thursday, 2 squirrels visited the feeder. On Friday, Gabrielle saw 5 squirrels at the feeder.

Squirrels at Bird Feeder

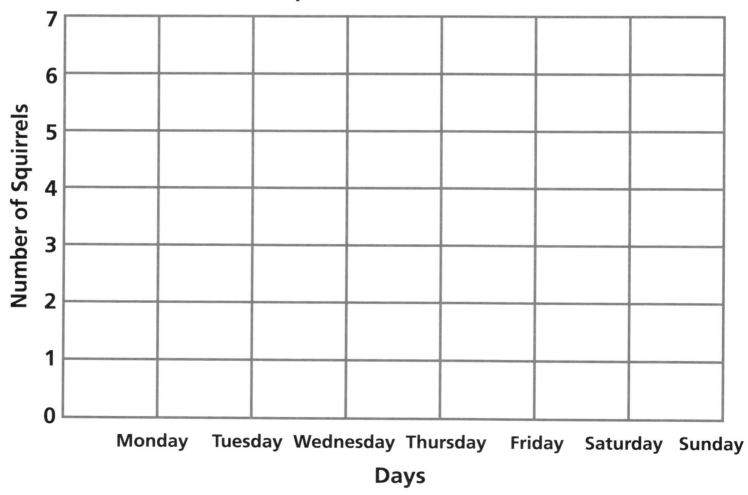

Number of Squirrels / Days: Monday, Tuesday, Wednesday, Thursday, Friday, Saturday, Sunday

Compare the Prices

Look at the prices of the toys below. Then answer the questions.

$3.20

$2.10

$2.50

$1.35

1. Golan bought a robot and building blocks for his sister. How much did he spend? _____

2. Izzy bought 2 items that cost $4.60 together. What did she buy?

_____

3. Benji bought two items. The total price of the items was $4.55. What did Benji buy? _____

4. Corin bought a teddy bear and a toy truck. How much did she spend in all? _____

Clothing Sale

Look at the prices of the items at the clothing sale.
Then answer the questions.

1. Owen spent $3.70. What items did he buy? _____

_____

2. Troy spent $4.70 on two items. He bought a shirt. What other

item did he buy? _____

3. Warren needs a new jacket and hat. How much would these items

cost him at the sale? _____

4. Which two clothing sale items add up to $5.50?

_____

Choose the Best Tool

Choose the best way to measure each item. Draw a line from the sentence on the left to the picture that finishes each sentence. Use each choice twice.

1. Measure the amount of lemonade with a _____.

2. Measure the length of the paperclip with a _____.

yard stick

3. Measure the weight of blueberries with a _____.

ruler

4. Measure the amount of water with a _____.

5. Measure the height of the tree with a _____.

 measuring cup

6. Measure the width of the book with a _____.

 scale

7. Measure the weight of the sand with a _____.

8. Measure the length of the car with a _____.

Time for School

Solve the problems.

1. It takes Eric 5 minutes to get dressed in the morning and 15 minutes to eat breakfast. He needs 10 minutes to pack his bookbag and brush his teeth. The school bus picks him up at 8:30. What is the latest Eric can wake up in the morning?

_____

2. Zooey walks to school each morning. It takes her 25 minutes to get there. She gets there a half hour early so she can get extra math help. If school starts at 9:00, what time must Zooey leave her home?

_____

3. It takes Viraj 20 minutes to walk to school each morning. Today he wants to stop for an extra 15 minutes along the way to visit his uncle's newsstand. If school starts at 9:00, what time must Dave leave home to visit his uncle and still get to school on time?

_____

4. School starts at 8:30. It ends at 2:30. How many hours are students in school during one day?

_____

How many hours are students in school during one week?

_____

On the Road

Solve the problems.

1. The Thomas family is taking a vacation. They have to drive 267 miles in all. They have already traveled 103 miles. How many miles do they have left on their trip?

_____

2. Mr. Thomas stops the car 3 times during the first 100 miles of the trip. Each time the car stops for 15 minutes. How many minutes does the car stop during the first 100 miles?

_____

3. The first part of the family trip is 56 miles. The second part is 33 miles. How many more miles will the family have to travel before they go a total of 100 miles?

_____

4. While on vacation, the Thomas family drives about 12 miles per day. How many days are they on vacation if they travel about 36 miles?

_____

Subtraction Action

Look at each set of numbers on the baseball caps.
Use the numbers to fill in the blanks in the number problems.
Use each number only once in a problem.

1.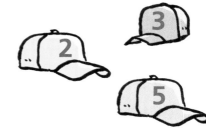

$$
\begin{array}{cc}
7 & \square \\
- \quad 2 & 1 \\
\hline
\square & \square
\end{array}
\qquad
\begin{array}{cc}
\square & 6 \\
- \quad \square & 4 \\
\hline
2 & \square
\end{array}
$$

2.

$$
\begin{array}{cc}
\square & \square \\
- \quad 3 & \square \\
\hline
1 & 8
\end{array}
\qquad
\begin{array}{cc}
\square & \square \\
- \quad 6 & 4 \\
\hline
2 & \square
\end{array}
$$

3.

$$
\begin{array}{cc}
\square & 7 \\
- \quad 2 & \square \\
\hline
\square & 2
\end{array}
\qquad
\begin{array}{cc}
\square & 6 \\
- \quad \square & \square \\
\hline
2 & 1
\end{array}
$$

4.

$$
\begin{array}{cc}
2 & \square \\
- \quad \square & 3 \\
\hline
\square & 3
\end{array}
\qquad
\begin{array}{cc}
9 & \square \\
- \quad 8 & \square \\
\hline
\square & 5
\end{array}
$$

Kite Flying

Use the numbers on each kite to make multiplication facts.
Write the facts to fill in the number sentences.

1.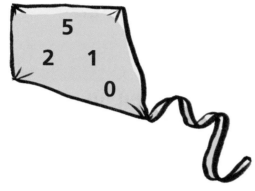

_____ × _____ = _____ _____

2.

_____ × _____ = _____ _____

3.

_____ × _____ = _____ _____

4.

_____ × _____ = _____ _____

5.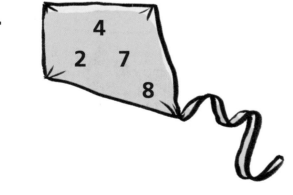

_____ × _____ = _____ _____

6.

_____ × _____ = _____ _____

Spelling Bee

The second-grade classes had a spelling bee. Read the tally chart to see how many times each class won. Then answer the questions below.

Classes That Won the Spelling Bee

Class	Tally
Mrs. Hall	卌 IIII
Ms. Gutierez	卌 I
Mr. Berkowitz	卌 III

1. Which class won the first-place ribbon in the spelling bee?

_____

2. How many more events did Mr. Berkowitz's class win than Ms. Gutierez's class?

_____

3. Which class won 8 spelling bee events?

_____

4. What kind of graph would best display the information in the tally chart?

_____

Around Town

The grid below is like a map. Points on the grid show places around town. Find the starting point. Follow the directions. Write the place where you go.

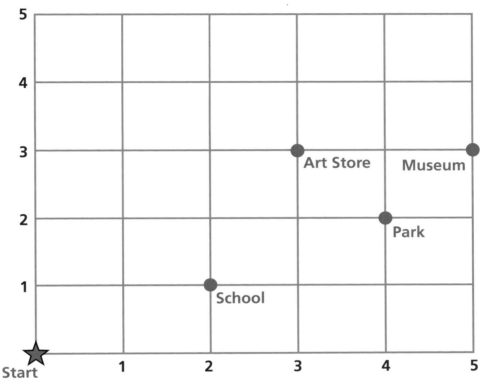

1. Go to the starting point. Go right 5. Go up 3. Where are you?

_____

2. Go to the starting point. Go up 1. Go right 2. Where are you?

_____

3. Go to the park. Go up 3. Go left 2. Go down 4. Where are you?

_____

4. Go to the starting point. Go up 5. Go right 4. Go down 3. Where are you? _____

5. You want to get to the same place you went in question 4. Write shorter directions to get you there. _____

_____

Science Fair

Read the story below about the science fair. Then solve the problems.

The school science fair is next week. The students must first take a science test. There were 7 students who scored 84. There were 4 students who scored 81. There were 3 students who scored 79. There were 3 students who scored 71.

1. How many students scored above 75 on their science test? _____

2. How many students scored below 75 on their test? _____

3. What is the median test score? _____

4. What is the range of test scores? _____

5. How many students scored above 80 on the test? _____

6. What was the total number of students who took the test? _____

On and Off the Bus

Solve the problems.

1. A bus has 6 people on it. Then 3 people get off the bus and 5 people get on. How many people are on the bus now?

_____

2. There are 12 people on the bus. Then 24 people get on and 5 get off. How many people are on the bus now?

_____

3. The bus makes 15 stops on its way uptown. Then it makes 13 stops on its way downtown. How many stops does the bus make in all as it drives around town?

_____

4. Mrs. Chang rides the bus 3 times every day, including weekends. How many times will Mrs. Chang ride the bus in one week?

_____

Addition Mission

Look at each set of numbers on the cars. Use the numbers to fill in the blanks in the number problems. Use each number only once in a problem.

1.

```
  7  0  ☐              ☐  ☐  3
+ 2  ☐  3           +  1  8  2
─────────           ──────────
  ☐  1  8              6  ☐  5
```

2.

```
  ☐  ☐  5              ☐  ☐  8
+ 1  0  1           +  6  1  0
─────────           ──────────
  4  ☐  6              9  ☐  8
```

3.

```
  ☐  3  0              6  2  6
+ 2  ☐  0           +  1  ☐  ☐
─────────           ──────────
  9  8  ☐              7  ☐  6
```

4.

```
  ☐  ☐  ☐              2  5  ☐
+ 2  2  2           +  4  2  1
─────────           ──────────
  6  8  9              ☐  ☐  5
```

Count Your Change

Look at each item below. Write the letter of the group of coins needed to buy it.

A

B

C

D

1.

_____

2.

_____

3.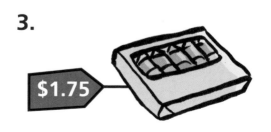

_____

4.

_____

5. Which group of coins shows the most money? _____

Bowling Bonanza

Gerry and his friends went bowling every week. Each time a person won a game, Gerry made a tally next to his or her name on his special chart. Use the chart to answer the questions.

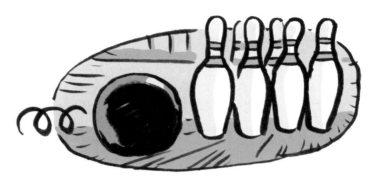

Bowling Winners

Name	Number of Wins
Akiko	IIII
Gerry	III
Lillian	~~IIII~~
Bobby	~~IIII~~
Sharie	~~IIII~~ II

1. How many games does the chart show? _____

2. Who won the most games? _____

3. What won the fewest games? _____

4. Which person had two fewer wins than Lillian? _____

5. Which person had 3 more wins than Akiko? _____

6. What is the range of scores for the group? _____

On the Farm

Read the story below about the new pigs on the farm.
Then answer the questions.

Many baby pigs were born on the farm this season. Seven of the pigs are 20 days old. Five of the pigs are 26 days old. Three pigs are 28 days old. Two pigs are 31 days old.

1. How many pigs were born on the farm this season? _____

2. How many pigs are less than 30 days old? _____

3. What is the median age of the pigs born this season? _____

4. What is the range of the ages of the pigs born this season? _____

5. How many more pigs are 20 days old than are 28 days old? _____

6. How many pigs are older than 27 days? _____

Fill in the Blanks

Look at each set of numbers in the boats. Use the numbers to fill in the blanks in the number problems. Use each number only once in a problem.

1.

```
  5 □ 3          □ 2 □
- 2 □ 1        - 3 □ 1
─────────      ─────────
  □ 4 2          1 2 2
```

2.

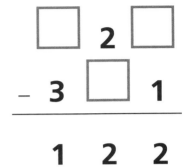

```
  7 7 □          9 1 8
- 6 □ 1        - 8 0 □
─────────      ─────────
  □ 6 4          □ □ 3
```

3.

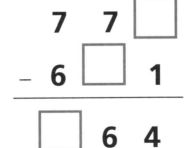
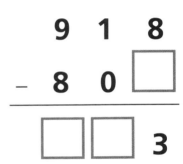

```
  □ 0 6          7 3 □
- 1 □ 4        - 5 3 1
─────────      ─────────
  1 0 □          □ □ 1
```

4.

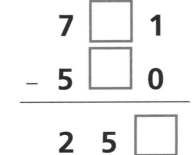
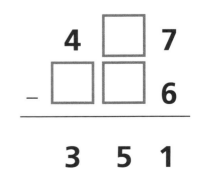

```
  7 □ 1          4 □ 7
- 5 □ 0        - □ □ 6
─────────      ─────────
  2 5 □          3 5 1
```

Math Books!

Use the numbers on each book to make multiplication facts. Write the facts to fill in the number sentences.

1.

_____ × _____ = _____ _____

2.

_____ × _____ = _____ _____

3.

_____ × _____ = _____ _____

4.

_____ × _____ = _____ _____

5.

_____ × _____ = _____ _____

6.

_____ × _____ = _____ _____

Farm Fresh Eggs

Solve the problems.

1. Each chicken at the Freshy Fresh Farm laid 3 eggs today. The farmer collected eggs from 8 chickens. How many eggs did the farmer collect in all? _____

2. The chickens on the farm eat a bag of seeds in the morning and two bags in the afternoon. How many bags of seeds will the chickens eat in a week? _____

3. Chickens at the farm lay white eggs and brown eggs. The farmer collects about 8 eggs of each color every day. How many eggs in all will the farmer collect in 5 days? _____

4. The farmer uses 3 eggs to make an omelet. How many eggs will it take for the farmer to make 9 omelets? _____

Cross Out

Make an **X** through the dollars or coins that are not needed to pay for each item shown.

1.  $1.06

2. $2.14

3.  $1.23

4.  $2.08

5. $1.80

At the Zoo

Solve the problems.

1. The dolphin show at the zoo is 20 minutes long. If the show starts at 2:30, what time will the show end? _____ How much extra time will there be before the 3:00 show? _____

2. The lions at the zoo eat at 4:30. It is 3:45. How long will it be before the lions eat? _____

3. The seals at the zoo get a small snack every half hour. How many snacks will they get from noon to 4:30? _____

4. The zoo opens at 9:00 in the morning and closes at 5:30 in the evening. How many hours is the zoo open in all? _____

_____

Inches or Feet?

Look at each picture.
Write **inches** or **feet** to estimate how long each item is.

1. **hand**   about 4 _____

2.  **pizza**   about 1 _____

3.  **lamp**   about 2 _____

4.  **table**   about 4 _____

5.  **tissue box**   about 7 _____

6.  **brick**   about 6 _____

Triangles Everywhere

Draw lines to make each shape into smaller triangles.

1.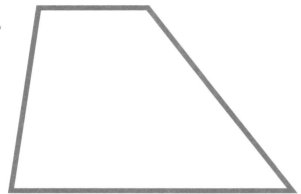

2.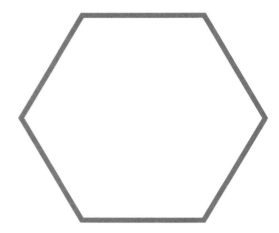

3.

4.

5.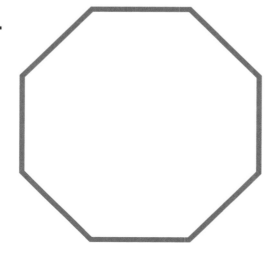

6.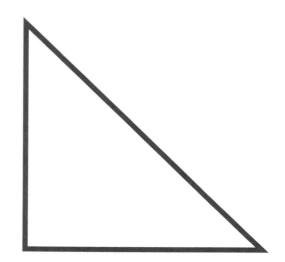

Measuring Weight

Write **ounces** or **pounds** to complete each sentence below. Choose the unit that makes the most sense.

1.

   Alexis's book weighs 5 _____.

2.

   Ingrid's bracelet weighs 2 _____.

3.

   Dan's football weighs about 14 _____.

4.

   Roberto's baby brother weighs about 15 _____.

5.

   The bird's nest weighs about 10 _____.

6.

   The fork weighs about 4 _____.

Raking Lawns

The line graph below shows the number of lawns raked each day for a week. Read the line graph. Then answer the questions.

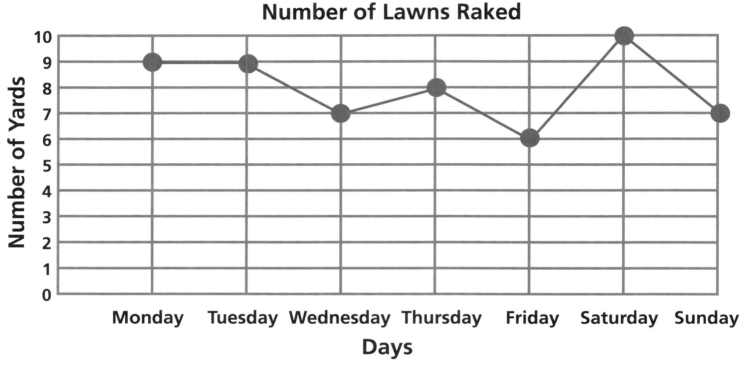

Number of Lawns Raked

1. How many lawns were raked on Saturday? _____

2. On which days were 7 lawns raked? _____

   _____

3. How many lawns in all were raked during the week?

   _____

4. How many lawns were raked during the weekend?

   _____

5. What is the median number of lawns raked? _____

6. Which two days would help you find the range of the data on the graph? _____ _____

Coin Combinations

Draw coins to show four different ways to make $1.50. Use only half dollars or quarters to draw your answers.

1.

2.

3.

4.

5. How many dimes are needed to make $1.50? _____

6. How many nickels are needed to make $1.50? _____

Bus Numbers

Use the numbers on each bus to make multiplication facts. Write the facts to fill in the number sentences.

1.

_____ × _____ = _____ _____

2.

_____ × _____ = _____ _____

3.

_____ × _____ = _____ _____

4.

_____ × _____ = _____ _____

5.

_____ × _____ = _____ _____

6.

_____ × _____ = _____ _____

At the Toy Store

Solve the problems.

1. The toy store sold 7 robots and 2 spaceships today. If they sell the same amount of space toys every day, how many space toys will they sell in one week?

_____

2. There are 5 shelves of dolls at the toy store. If there are 9 dolls on each shelf, how many dolls are in the store in all?

_____

3. Each race car in the store has 4 wheels. How many wheels are there in all if there are 5 race cars?

_____

4. The beach balls at the store cost 3 dollars each. How much would a customer spend on 8 beach balls?

_____

Rainy Days

The line graph below shows the number of inches it rained each day last week. Read the graph. Then answer the questions.

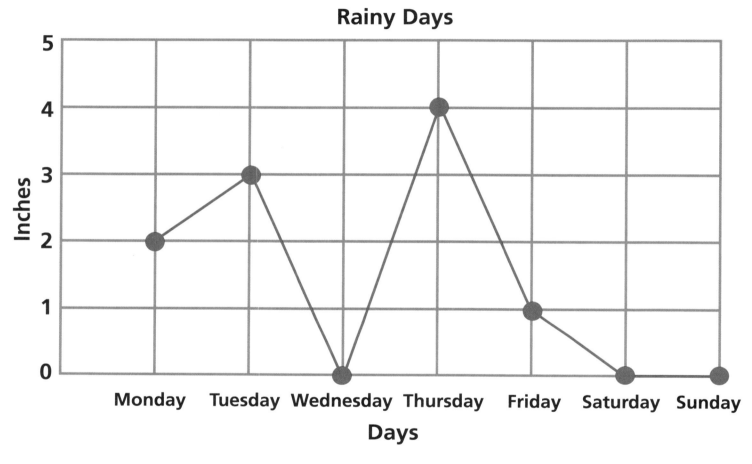

1. How many days did it rain last week? _____

2. On what day did it rain 4 inches? _____

3. What is the range of inches it rained last week?

_____

4. How many more inches did it rain on Thursday than it did on Friday? _____

5. How many inches did it rain in all last week?

_____

A Day at the Fair

The grid below is like a map. Points on the grid show where activities are found at the fair. Write directions to get from the starting point to each point on the map.

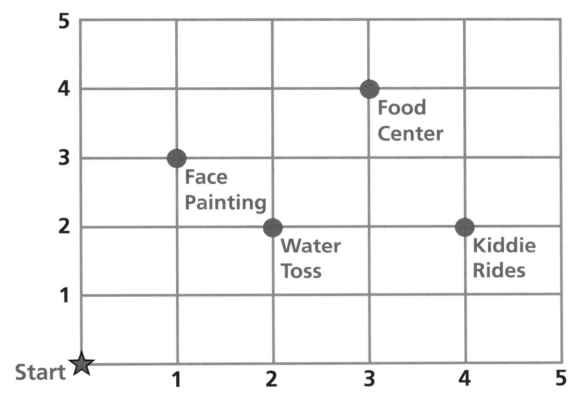

1. Face Painting

_____

2. Water Toss

_____

3. Food Center

_____

4. Kiddie Rides

_____

Price Riddles

Look at the price of each item.
Then answer the questions below.

A OATS $1.26

B MORNING MIX $1.00

C Blueberry Berries $1.35

1. Which box of cereal can be paid for with just 2 coins? _____

2. If you bought a cereal with 1 dollar bill and 1 half dollar, which one would you get the least amount of change back from?

_____

3. You use exact change to pay for a box of cereal. For which box would you need 1 dollar bill, 1 quarter, and only 1 penny? _____

4. You have only 92 cents. How much more money would you need to buy a box of Oats? _____

5. The price of the boxes of cereal has gone up 12 cents. How much are the Blueberry Berries now? _____

Write It Three Ways

Write each amount in three different ways. You can use dollar bills, half dollars, quarters, dimes, nickels, and pennies.

1. $1.22

_____

_____

_____

2. $1.50

_____

_____

_____

3. $1.12

_____

_____

_____

4. $1.46

_____

_____

_____

County Fair

Help the judges find the biggest pig at the county fair.
Use the clues to find out the weight of each pig below.

Kenneth   **Patty**   **Scott**   **Becky Sue**

Kenneth's pig is 62 pounds. Becky Sue's pig is 24 pounds bigger than Kenneth's. Scott's pig is 15 pounds bigger than Becky Sue's. Patty's pig is 35 pounds lighter than Becky Sue's.

1. Patty's pig is _____ pounds.

2. Scott's pig is _____ pounds.

3. Becky Sue's pig is _____ pounds.

4. Whose pig will win the blue ribbon for being the biggest? _____

Moon and Stars

Use the numbers on the stars to make multiplication facts. Write the facts to fill in the number sentences.

1.

3   2   7   1

_____ × _____ = _____ _____

2.

6   4   8   8

_____ × _____ = _____ _____

3.

6   2   4   4

_____ × _____ = _____ _____

4.

5   5   5   2

_____ × _____ = _____ _____

5.

4   8   6   8

_____ × _____ = _____ _____

6.

8   4   2   7

_____ × _____ = _____ _____

Popcorn Graph

The line graph below shows the number of bags of popcorn sold during a baseball game. Read the line graph. Then answer the questions.

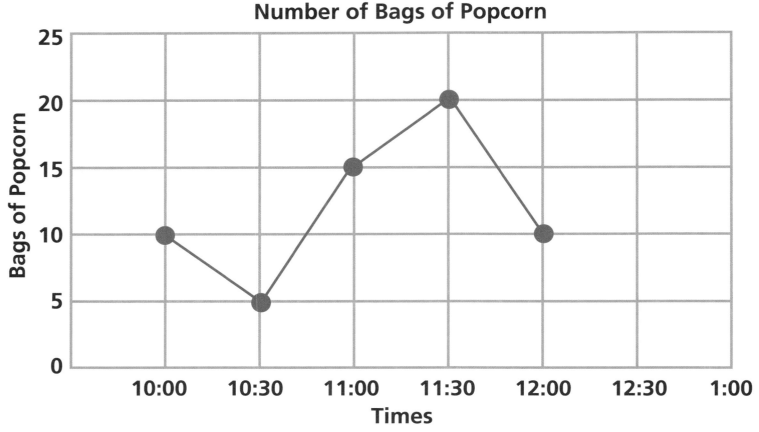

Number of Bags of Popcorn

1. How many bags of popcorn were sold at 10:30? _____

2. At what time were the most bags of popcorn sold? _____

3. How many more bags of popcorn were sold at 12:00 than were sold at 10:30? _____

4. If 5 bags of popcorn were sold at 12:30, would the line on the graph go up or down? _____

5. No bags of popcorn were sold at 1:00. Which line on the graph will get a dot? _____

My Neighborhood

The grid below is like a map. Points on the grid show where houses in a neighborhood are. Write directions to get from the starting point to each point on the map.

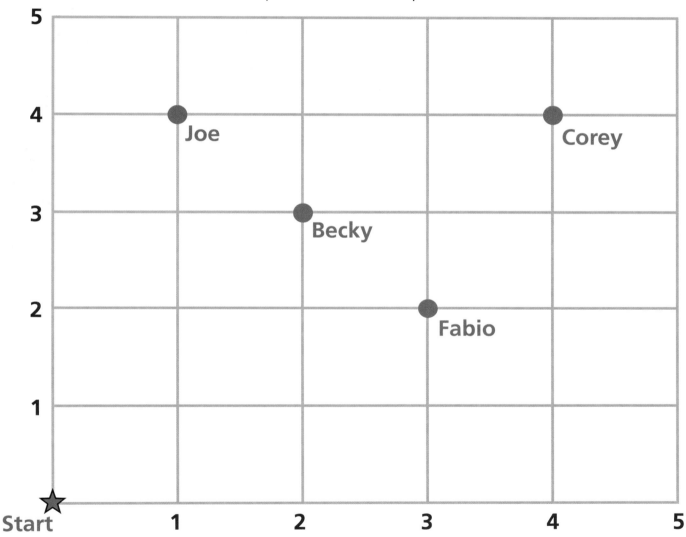

1. Joe's house _____

2. Becky's house _____

3. Fabio's house _____

4. Corey's house _____

Garden Fractions

Solve the problems.

1. Grandma planted tomatoes in $\frac{1}{2}$ of the garden. Grandpa planted peppers in $\frac{1}{4}$ of the garden. How much of the garden is left for planting? _____

2. Molly picked $\frac{2}{3}$ of the vegetables in the garden. What fraction of the vegetables are left? _____

3. Grandma and Grandpa planted a total of 12 kinds of vegetables. Write a fraction to describe half of the vegetables in the garden.

   _____

4. How many kinds of vegetables would Grandma need to pick if she wants to make a salad that has $\frac{1}{3}$ of the different vegetables in her garden? _____

Draw the Solid

Follow the directions to draw each solid figure.

1. Draw a figure that has a circle as one face.

2. Draw a figure that has a circle as two faces.

3. Draw a figure that has the same shape on all faces.

4. Draw a figure that has a square as one shape.

5. Draw a figure that has a rectangle on all sides.

6. Write a sentence to describe this figure.

_____

_____

_____

In the Classroom

Jim, Craig, Brendan, Josh, and Mark are sitting at a baseball game. Use the clues in the box below to find out the order that each boy is sitting in on the bleachers. Then write their names under their pictures.

Mark is sitting between Brendan and Jim.

Jim is sitting to the left of Craig.

Brendan is sitting to the right of Josh.

How Much Does It Weigh?

Solve the problems.

1. Ray and Mona used the scale at the grocery store. Ray bought a carrot that was 8 ounces. Mona bought an apple that was 5 ounces. There are 16 ounces in a pound. How many more ounces of food must they buy to reach a pound of food? _____

2. Bradley weighs 59 pounds. His little sister weighs 31 pounds. How many more pounds does Bradley weigh than his sister? _____

3. Mom's new flowerpot weighs 88 ounces with the plant and soil in it. The pot weighs 16 ounces by itself. How much do the soil and plant weigh? _____

4. Rick's new bicycle weighs 38 pounds. The wheels weigh 12 pounds. How much does the rest of the bicycle weigh without the wheels? _____

Coin Collecting

Draw coins to show six different ways to make $1.10. You may use quarters, dimes, and nickels in your drawings.

1.

2.

3.

4.

5.

6.

Colorful Clothes!

Look at the patterns on the clothes below. Complete each pattern by coloring the rest of the shirts in the row.

1.

2.

3.

4.

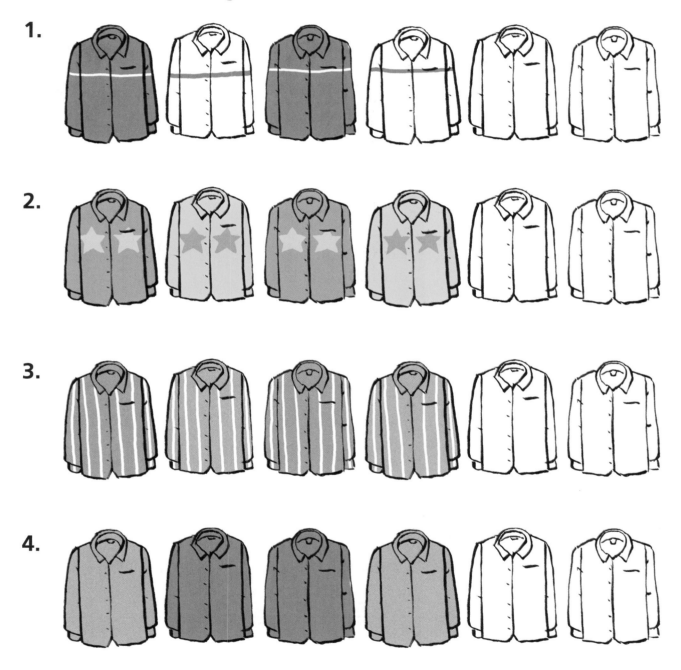

Number Sentences

Write a number sentence that will solve each problem. You do not have to solve the problem. Use a box to show where the answer to the number sentence belongs.

1. Each peacock at the zoo has 19 feathers. Write a number sentence to show how many feathers 4 peacocks at the zoo have.

_____

2. There are 36 seats at the dolphin show, 21 seats at the python show, and 20 seats at the elephant show. Write a number sentence to show how many seats there are in all of the shows combined.

_____

3. There are 48 seats at the tiger show and 34 of those seats are filled. How many seats at the tiger show are not filled?

_____

4. The zoo had 357 visitors today. They had 213 visitors yesterday. How many more visitors were at the zoo today than yesterday?

_____

Choose Your Lunch

The school is serving a sandwich, soup, salad, or stew for lunch. Each child can choose two servings of food as his or her lunch. Each can choose two servings of the same food, or each can choose one serving of two different foods. Write the name of the foods on the plates to show how the foods can be combined.

Playground Fractions

Solve the problems.

1. There are 12 swings at the park. Three of the swings are baby swings. What fraction of the swings at the park are baby swings?

_____

2. Twenty-four children went down the slide in the past hour. What fraction describes that 12 of the children were girls? _____

3. The climbing wall at the park is 15 feet high. How many feet did Jedediah climb if he climbed $\frac{1}{3}$ the height of the wall? _____

4. The park has 9 different pieces of equipment for kids to play on. Emily played on $\frac{1}{3}$ of the pieces of equipment today. What fraction of the equipment has Emily not yet played on? _____

Fold 'em Up!

Draw a line from each shape on the left to the folded shape on the right that matches it.

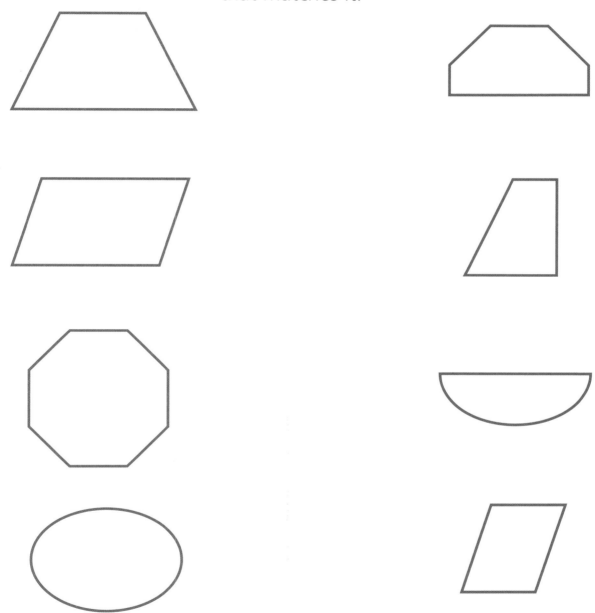

Draw what this shape would look like after it has been folded in half.

Lemonade, Iced Tea!

Jordon and Bethany are selling lemonade and iced tea at the baseball game. Use the clues in the box below to find out how many drinks they sold today. Write **cannot tell** if there are not enough clues to answer a question.

They sold twice as many cups of lemonade as they sold cups of iced tea.

They sold twice as many lemonades as last week.

They gave away 100 straws last week to go with every cup of lemonade they sold.

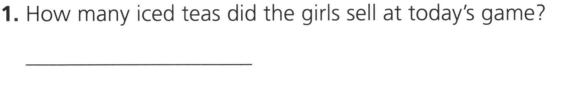

1. How many iced teas did the girls sell at today's game?

_____

2. How many iced teas did the girls sell at last week's game?

_____

3. How many lemonades did the girls sell at today's game?

_____

4. How many lemonades did the girls sell at last week's game?

_____

5. How many drinks did the girls sell this week in all?

_____

Fun at Camp

Solve the problems.

1. There are 46 campers at Camp Funshine. Of the campers, 30 were at the relay races yesterday. How many campers did not attend the relay races? _____

2. Each camper gets three chances at the ring toss. If there are 8 campers at the ring toss, how many tosses will there be in all? _____

3. Riley swam 9 laps on Monday and 7 laps on Tuesday. On Wednesday he swam the amount that he swam on Monday and Tuesday combined. How many laps did Riley swim in the first three days of the week? _____

4. There will be 5 baseball games this week at camp. If Jose makes 3 home runs during every game, how many home runs will he make this week at camp? _____

Watch the Weather

The weather can be sunny, windy, rainy, or cold. Most days it is a combination of these different kinds of weather. Write all of the combinations of two different kinds of weather in the clouds below.

Alphabet Patterns

Look at each letter pattern below. Then finish the pattern.

1. R, G, W, R, G, W, R,

____, ____, ____, ____, ____, ____, ____, ____

2. T, T, U, U, U, V, V, V, V,

____, ____, ____, ____, ____, ____, ____, ____

3. X, X, Y, Y, Z, Z, A, A, B, B,

____, ____, ____, ____, ____, ____, ____, ____

4. Y, Y, E, E, S, S, Y, Y,

____, ____, ____, ____, ____, ____, ____, ____

5. L, M, M, N, N, N, O, O, O, O,

____, ____, ____, ____, ____, ____, ____, ____

Count It Out!

Make an **X** through the dollars or coins that are not needed to pay for each item shown.

1.  $1.25

2. $1.60

3. $2.50

4.  $1.33

5. $1.75

Racing through the Market

Guess the length of each animal's path through the supermarket. Write your guess on the chart that says **Guess**. Then measure each path with a ruler. Write the actual length on the chart that says **Check**.

Guess	Check

Which Giraffe?

Solve the riddles. Write the letter of the giraffe that is being described.

1. It does not have a hat.
It is not made of one color.
Which is it?

_____

2. It is wearing a hat.
It is not wearing green.
Which is it?

_____

3. It is made of just one color.
It is wearing a hat that
matches its fur.
Which is it?

_____

4. It is a solid color.
It is not wearing a hat.
Which is it?

_____

Jogging Time!

The children in Corner School are practicing for relay races at the school picnic. The line graph below shows the number of minutes children in each grade must spend each day running. Read the line graph. Then answer the questions.

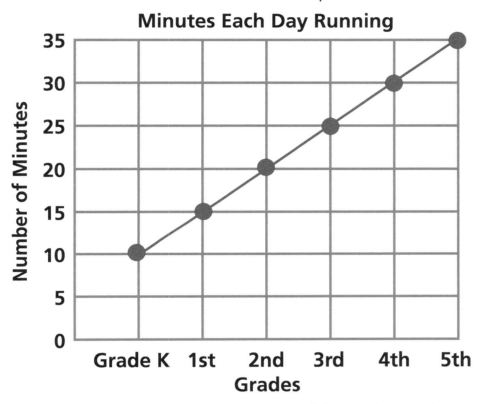

Minutes Each Day Running

1. How much extra running must children do each year?

   _____

2. How many more minutes must a fifth grader practice than a kindergartner?_____

3. How many minutes do you predict a sixth grader would have to practice each day?_____

4. How can you describe the pattern shown in the graph?

   _____

Where's the Center?

Write the letter of the line that shows the middle of the shape.

1.

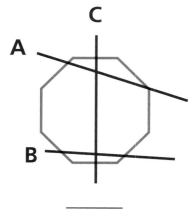

_____

2.

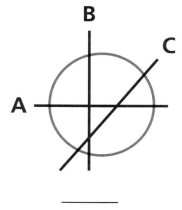

_____

3.

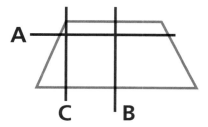

_____

4.

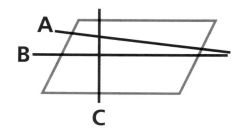

_____

5.

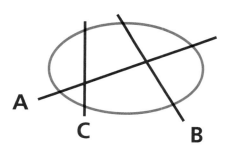

_____

6.

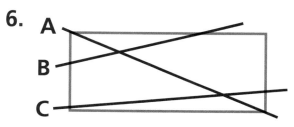

_____

Out for a Spin

What will happen when Laura takes a turn with the spinner? Look at each spinner in the table below. Write the name of the color that the spinner is most likely and least likely to land on.

	Most Likely	Least Likely
1.		
2.		
3.		
4.		

Fun in the Snow

Solve the problems.

1. Jordanna makes a snowman out of 3 large balls of snow. How many snowballs will Jordanna have to make if she wants to make 8 snowmen? _____

2. The sledding hill in Julio's neighborhood is 21 feet long. Julio sleds down the hill 3 times. How many feet does Julio sled in all? _____

3. It snowed 7 inches on Thursday and 11 inches on Friday. Then it snowed another inch on Saturday. How many inches did it snow in all on Thursday through Saturday? _____

4. Esther makes 45 snowballs for a snowball fight. Jessica makes 56 snowballs for the snowball fight. How many more snowballs did Jessica make for the snowball fight? _____

What Can I Buy?

What can you buy with each set of bills and coins? Write the name of the item on the line.

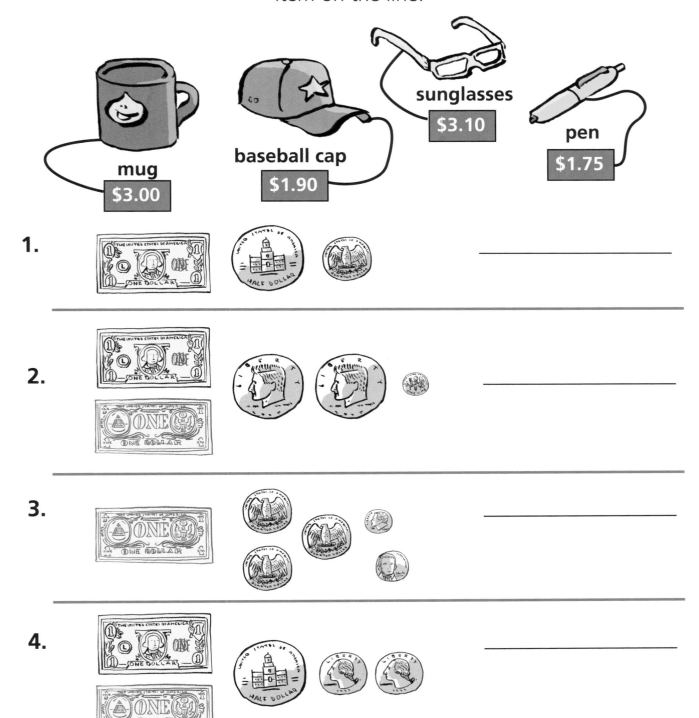

mug
$3.00

baseball cap
$1.90

sunglasses
$3.10

pen
$1.75

1. _____

2. _____

3. _____

4. _____

Time in the Garden

Solve the problems.

1. Tunde has to plant seeds in the garden. It takes him about 15 minutes to plant each type of vegetable. How long will it take Tunde to plant the seeds if he plants 5 different kinds of vegetables? _____

2. The new garden must be watered with the sprinkler for 20 minutes each day. If the sprinkler is used for exactly one hour each week, on how many days is it run?

_____

3. It will take 3 weeks for Tunde's vegetable plants to grow flowers. How many days are in three weeks?

_____

4. Tunde started weeding his garden at 3:30. It is now 4:25. For how long has Tunde been weeding his garden?

_____

Color the Backpacks

Megan has 8 backpacks in her closet. Each is a solid color. The backpacks are orange, yellow, blue, and red. Use the clues in the box below to color the backpacks.

> There are more blue backpacks than any other color.
>
> There are twice as many yellow backpacks as red backpacks.
>
> There are the same number of yellow and orange backpacks.

My Map

The grid below is like a map. Points on the grid show places a person can go in a neighborhood. Make your own neighborhood by putting four dots on the map. Then write directions to describe how to get to each place.

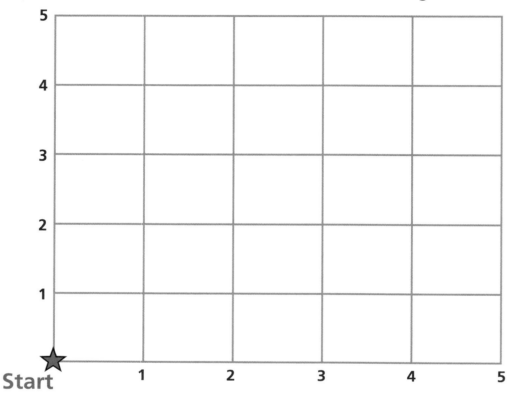

1. Location 1 is the _____. You can get there by going

_____.

2. Location 2 is the _____. You can get there by going

_____.

3. Location 3 is the _____. You can get there by going

_____.

4. Location 4 is the _____. You can get there by going

_____.

Tell Me Why

One of the shapes in each group does not belong. Make an **X** through the shape. Then explain why it does not belong.

1.

_____

_____

2.

_____

_____

3.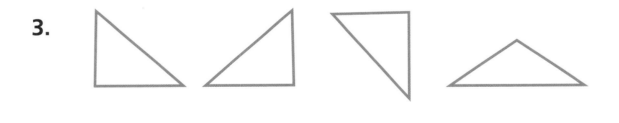

_____

_____

4.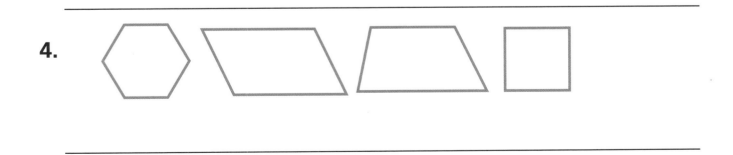

_____

_____

Draw the Money

Read each clue, then draw the correct coins. Show half dollars, quarters, dimes, and nickels.

1. There are 5 coins. They add up to $1.05.

2. There are 4 coins. They add up to $1.35.

3. There are 9 coins. They add up to $1.90.

4. There are 3 coins. They add up to $1.50.

How Heavy?

Solve the problems.

1. There are 16 ounces in one pound. How many pounds and ounces does Glenn's baseball-card collection weigh if it weighs 29 ounces? _____

2. Each of Glenn's baseball cards weighs about a half ounce. About how many cards will there be in a pile of cards that weighs one pound? _____

3. Glenn's brother has a baseball-card collection that weighs about 18 ounces. How many more ounces should his collection be to make it equal to Glenn's 29-ounce collection? _____

4. Glenn stepped on a bathroom scale carrying a big box of baseball cards. The scale read 68 pounds. If Glenn weighs 52 pounds, how much does the box weigh? _____

In the Lunchroom

Students were assigned seats in the cafeteria during lunchtime. Use the clues in the box below to write each student's name in the place where he or she will sit.

Elena sits in front of the window.

Pedro sits in a corner.

Elena sits across from Carter.

Yoko sits to Carter's right.

Kyle sits to Elena's right.

Hanna sits across from Kyle.

Fold It Up!

Draw a line from the shape in the left column to the folded shape that matches it on the right.

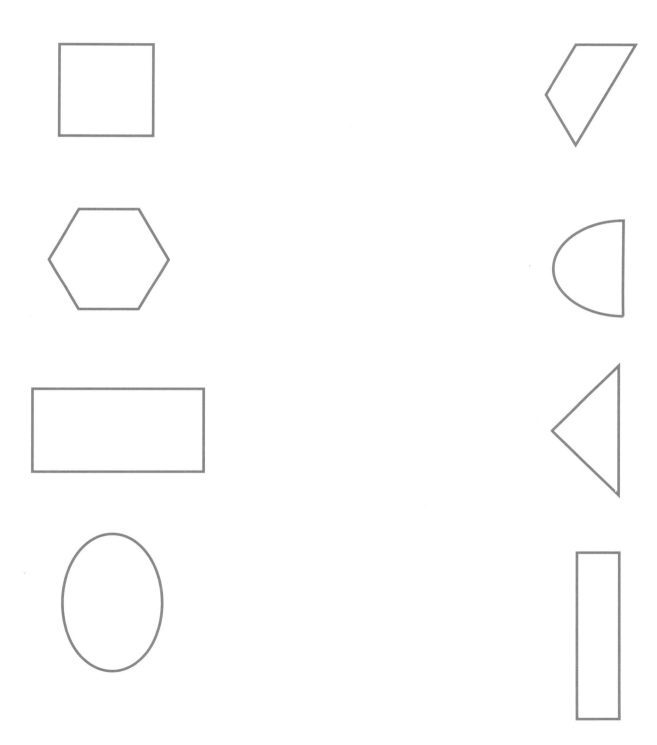

Too Much Money!

Make an **X** through the dollars or coins that are not needed to pay for each item shown.

1.  **$1.15**

2.  **$1.45**

3.  **$2.20**

4.  **$1.11**

5.  **$1.58**

Find the Face

Follow the directions below.

1. Circle the figure that has a square face.

2. Circle the figure that has a round face.

3. Circle the figure that has a rectangular face.

4. Draw a pyramid. Then draw the separate shapes that make up the pyramid.

Back in Time

Look at each clock. Write the time that it was two and a half hours before.

1.

_____

2.

_____

3.

_____

4.

_____

5.

_____

6.

_____

Which Fish?

Solve the riddles. Write the letter of the fish that is being described.

1. It does not have a hat.

It likes jewelry.

Which is it? _____

2. It is the color of the sea.

It is not wearing anything.

Which is it? _____

3. It is made of two colors.

It likes to wear hats.

Which is it? _____

4. It is not a solid color.

It cannot see well.

Which is it? _____

Froggy Fever

There are 8 frogs on a log. Some frogs are solid green and some are solid brown. Others are green with brown spots. Some are brown with green spots. Color the frogs to match the clues in the box below.

There are more solid green frogs than any other kind.

There are twice as many brown frogs with green spots as green frogs with brown spots.

There are the same number of brown frogs and brown frogs with green spots.

How Much Is It?

What can you buy with each set of bills and coins? Write the name of the item on the line.

$2.50 Orange Juice $3.20 Magazine   Tissues $1.98   Toy Car $2.60

1.

_____

2.

_____

3.

_____

4.

_____

The Longest Ribbons

Use the clues below to find out which of the girls has the longest ribbons.

Eileen　　**Shirley**　　**Maureen**　　**Colleen**

Eileen's ribbons are two feet long. Shirley's ribbons are half the length of Eileen's ribbons. Colleen's ribbons are 6 inches longer than Shirley's. Maureen's ribbons are 4 inches longer than Eileen's.

1. Colleen's ribbons are _____ inches long.

2. Shirley's ribbons are _____ inches long.

3. Maureen's ribbons are _____ inches long.

4. Eileen's ribbons are _____ inches long.

Baseball Card Fractions

Solve the problems.

1. Jane has 21 baseball cards. One-third of the cards show members of her favorite team. How many cards show her favorite team?

_____

2. Donnie has 30 baseball cards. One-tenth of his cards are doubles. How many of his cards are doubles? _____

3. Ethan buys 12 baseball cards. He gives $\frac{1}{2}$ of them to his sister. How many cards does Ethan give to his sister? _____

4. Javier's baseball collection has 6 cards in it. The collection is $\frac{1}{2}$ the size of Raj's collection. How many cards does Raj have in his collection? _____

When Did That Happen?

Read each problem. Write the time on the clock.

1. It is 7:45. Pilar should have been home 3 hours ago. What time should Pilar have been home?

2. Elaine has 20 more minutes left of homework to do. Right now it is 4:30. What time will Elaine be finished with her homework?

3. The movie is starting right now. It is 2 hours and 15 minutes long. If it is 3:00 now, what time will the movie be over?

4. Uncle Chace has been at the store for 45 minutes. It is 11:30. What time did Uncle Chace get to the store?

Guess That Number

Solve the riddles below. Use the numbers 0 to 9 to write the correct two-digit numbers on the flowers below.

1. The sum of the digits is 16. Their difference is 0. The number is even.

2. The sum of the digits is 12. Their difference is 6. The number is odd.

3. The sum of the digits is 9. Their difference is 5. The number is even.

4. The sum of the digits is 11. Their difference is 1. The number is odd.

5. The sum of the digits is 9. Their difference is 1. The number is even.

6. The sum of the digits is 3. Their difference is 1. The number is odd.

Answer Key

Page 4
1. Circle 823 and move it to the end of the line.
2. Circle 233 and move it to the beginning of the line.
3. Circle 426 and move it right after 401.
4. Circle 999 and move it to the end of the line.

Page 5
Possible answers include:
573, 537, 735, 753, 375, 357
These are the numbers in order from greatest to least:
753, 735, 573, 537, 375, 357

Page 6
1. 109, 111, 113
2. 430, 425, 420
3. 215, 218, 221
4. 371, 381, 391
5. 730, 732, 734

Page 7
Possible answers for questions 1–6 include:
1 half dollar, 1 quarter
1 half dollar, 2 dimes, 1 nickel
3 quarters
2 quarters, 2 dimes, 1 nickel
1 quarter, 5 dimes
1 quarter, 3 dimes, 4 nickels
7. 15

Page 8
1. 3,408; three thousand four hundred eight
2. 783; seven hundred eighty-three
3. 9,070; nine thousand seventy
4. 639; six hundred thirty-nine
5. 1,133; one thousand one hundred thirty-three
6. 428; four hundred twenty-eight

Page 9
1. Circle 408 and move it before 406.
2. Circle 777 and move to the beginning of the line.
3. Circle 131 and move to the end of the line.
4. Circle 379 and move it before 368.

Page 10
Possible answers include:
915, 951, 519, 591, 195, 159
These are the numbers in order from least to greatest:
159, 195, 519, 591, 915, 951

Page 11
Possible answer for questions 1-6 include:
1 half dollar, 1 quarter, 1 nickel
1 half dollar, 3 dimes
3 quarters, 1 nickel
1 quarter, 5 dimes, 1 nickel
4 dimes, 8 nickels
8 dimes

Page 12
1. 75 cents
2. 2 quarters, 2 dimes, 1 nickel
3. 3
4. 75¢

Page 13
1. 95 cents
2. $1.10
3. $1.35
4. Rebecca
5. Mike

Page 14
1. inches
2. feet
3. inch
4. feet
5. feet
6. Answers will vary. Possible answers include: a piece of paper, a book, a ruler.

Page 15
1. yards
2. feet
3. feet
4. yards
5. feet
6. yards
7. feet
8. yards

Page 16
1. 4:40
2. 7:20
3. 8:50
4. 2:25
5. 9:45
6. 5:05

Page 17
Answers will vary depending on predictions and actual measurements of time.

Page 18
1. square
2. rectangle
3. rectangle
4. circle
5. circle
6. square

Page 19
1. triangle; The triangle is the only shape with edges and vertices.
2. oval; The oval is the only shape with no edges or vertices.
3. trapezoid; The trapezoid is the only shape with sides that are not parallel.
4. scalene triangle; The scalene triangle is the only one with an obtuse angle.

Page 20
1.
There were 2 red trains and 8 blue trains.

2.
There were 4 red trains and 4 blue trains.

3.
There were 3 red trains and 6 blue trains.

Page 21
1. red
2. orange
3. 3
4. blue

Page 22
1. red: $\frac{1}{4}$
   blue: $\frac{3}{4}$
2. yellow: $\frac{2}{6}$
   purple: $\frac{4}{6}$
3. yellow: $\frac{3}{6}$
   green: $\frac{2}{6}$
   red: $\frac{1}{6}$
4. gray: $\frac{1}{3}$
   blue: $\frac{2}{3}$
5. white: $\frac{2}{4}$
   orange: $\frac{2}{4}$
6. yellow: $\frac{1}{8}$
   blue: $\frac{5}{8}$
   red: $\frac{2}{8}$

Page 23
1. Star will have 3 sections colored green, 2 sections colored red.
2. Flower will have 4 yellow petals, 2 blue petals, 2 green petals.
3. Snowflake will have 1 blue section, 3 yellow sections.
4. Clover will have 1 orange section and 2 blue sections.
5. Orange will have 2 purple sections and 2 red sections.
6. Flower will have 1 orange section, 2 green sections, 2 purple sections.

Page 24
1. $1.15
2. $1.10
3. $1.35
4. Jake

Page 25
1. 79
2. 29
3. 37
4. 16

Page 26
1. +; −
2. −; +
3. +; +
4. −; +
5. −; −
6. +; −
7. +; −
8. −; +

Page 27
1. 46 + 51 = 97
   65 + 22 = 87
2. 28 + 61 = 89
   17 + 21 = 38
3. 43 + 15 = 58
   24 + 54 = 78
4. 77 + 22 = 99
   72 + 20 = 92

Page 28
1. ▭
2. ○
3. ○
4. ⬡
5. △
6. △

Page 29
1. increase by 100
2. decrease by 100
3. increase by 10
4. decrease by 10
5. increase by 111

Page 30
1.
2.
3.
4.

Page 31
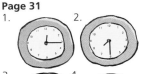

Page 32
1. pounds
2. ounces
3. pounds
4. ounces
5. ounces
6. ounces
7. ounces
8. pounds

Page 33

	First Grade	Second Grade	Third Grade
Susie	X	Yes	X
Sandy	X	X	Yes
Carrie	Yes	X	X

1. Carrie
2. Susie
3. Sandy

Page 34
1. 21
2. 9
3. 21
4. 15

Page 35

Page 36
Webby; Quacker; Billy; Waddles; Feathers

Page 37
1. 44
2. 24; 24
3. 6; 16; 22
4. 30

Page 38
1. 2 dollar bills, 1 dime, 1 nickel, 1 penny
2. 4 dollar bills, 2 half dollars, 2 quarters
3. 2 dollar bills, 1 quarter, 1 dime, 3 pennies
4. 2 dollar bills, 1 quarter, 1 nickel
5. 1 dollar bill, 1 quarter, 1 dime, 2 nickels, 1 penny
6. 3 dollar bills, 1 nickel, 2 pennies

Page 39
1. $1.50
2. $1.82
3. 60 cents
4. $1.82
5. $3.80
6. $1.75

Page 40
1. 29
2. 5
3. 5
4. 5
5. 14
6. soccer

Page 41
1. green: $\frac{1}{4}$
   orange: $\frac{3}{4}$
2. blue: $\frac{2}{4}$
   red: $\frac{2}{4}$
3. purple: $\frac{1}{3}$
   red: $\frac{2}{3}$
4. yellow: $\frac{3}{8}$
   orange: $\frac{5}{8}$

Page 42
1. 17
2. 8
3. 9
4. 5
5. 3
6. 6

Page 43
1–3.

4. Wednesday
5. 4

Page 44

	Spaghetti	Hamburgers	Chicken
Friday	X	Yes	X
Saturday	X	X	Yes
Sunday	Yes	X	X

1. hamburgers
2. chicken
3. spaghetti

Page 45
1. seconds
2. minutes
3. minutes
4. hours
5. hours

Page 46
1. 9 feet
2. 13 feet
3. 11 feet
4. 16 feet

Page 47
1. 2 dollar bills, 1 quarter, 1 dime, 2 pennies
2. 2 dollar bills, 4 quarters
3. 3 dollar bills, 1 half dollar, 1 quarter, 1 penny
4. 2 dollar bills, 2 half dollars, 1 quarter
5. 2 dollar bills, 1 quarter, 1 nickel, 3 pennies
6. 1 bill, 4 quarters, 2 dimes

Page 48
1. 279; 972
2. 136; 631
3. 478; 874
4. 259; 952
5. 238; 832
6. 246; 642

Page 49
1. 41
2. 82
3. 77
4. 62
5. 53
6. 90

Page 50
1. 24
2. 3
3. 60
4. 500

Page 51
1. −; +
2. +; +
3. −; −
4. +; −
5. +; −
6. +; +
7. −; −
8. +; −

Page 52
1.

2.

3.

4.

5.

Page 53
1. 790, 800, 810, 820
   increase by 10
2. 400, 350, 300, 250
   decrease by 50
3. 500, 480, 460, 440
   decrease by 20
4. 175, 200, 225, 250
   increase by 25
5. 206, 212, 218, 224
   increase by 6

Page 54
Possible pairs include:
orange/orange
brown/brown
yellow/yellow
blue/blue
orange/brown
orange/yellow
orange/blue
brown/yellow
brown/blue
yellow/blue

Page 55

Most Likely	Least Likely
red	blue
blue	green
red	orange
orange	red

Page 56

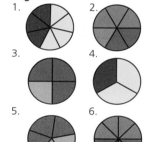

Page 57
1. $\frac{1}{12}$
2. $\frac{2}{12}$
3. $\frac{5}{12}$
4. 6
5. 3
6. 4

Page 58
1. 5
2. 4
3. 10
4. 16
5. 8
6. 4

Page 59
1. rectangular prism
2. sphere
3. cone
4. triangular prism
5. A cube and a rectangle have the same number of faces, edges, and vertices.

Page 60
Four-digit numbers include:
1,248; 1,284; 1,428; 1,482; 1,824; 1,842; 2,148; 2,184; 2,481; 2,418; 2,814; 2,841; 4,128; 4,182; 4,218;

4,281; 4,812; 4,821; 8,124; 8,142; 8,214; 8,241; 8,412; 8,421

Page 61
1. 73
2. 62
3. 88
4. 42
5. 21
6. 65

Page 62
1. 76
2. 333
3. 42
4. 754

Page 63
1. 54, 58, 62, 66
   increase by 4
2. 713, 711, 709, 707
   decrease by 2
3. 55, 50, 45, 40
   decrease by 5
4. 90, 105, 120, 135
   increase by 15
5. 520, 620, 720, 820
   increase by 100
6. Patterns and rules will vary.

Page 64
Combinations of shirts and pants include:
blue shirt/blue pants
blue shirt/black pants
blue shirt/brown pants
green shirt/blue pants
green shirt/black pants
green shirt/brown pants
red shirt/blue pants
red shirt/black pants
red shirt/brown pants

Page 65
1. 1 face, 0 edges, 1 vertex
2. 6 faces, 12 edges, 8 vertices
3. 0 faces, 0 edges, 0 vertices
4. 5 faces, 9 edges, 6 vertices
5. 6 faces, 12 edges, 8 vertices
6. 2 faces, 0 edges, 0 vertices

Page 66
1. Henry
2. Lesia
3. Milo
4. Rita
5. Robot drawing should have square body, square head, oval arms and legs, triangular ears, and rectangular feet.

Page 67
1.

2.

3.

4.

5.

Page 68
1. $\frac{3}{16}$ 2. 8
3. 4 4. $\frac{7}{16}$
5. $\frac{1}{16}$ 6. $\frac{10}{16}$

Page 69
1. 5 2. $\frac{1}{5}$
3. $\frac{10}{20}$ 4. 10
5. $\frac{2}{5}$ 6. $\frac{4}{20}$

Page 70
Ashley; Jen; Katie; Amrita; Alicia

Page 71

Page 72
1. How many baseball cards do Jeff and Tony have in all?
2. How much money do the girls have altogether?
3. How many laps does Darren swim in 5 days?
4. How many pies did Mom leave at home?

Page 73
1. Roy
2. Mary
3. Javier
4. Rico

Page 74
1. 30 minutes
2. reading
3. a half hour
4. 45 minutes
5. circle time
6. reading

Page 75
1. feet 2. inches
3. foot 4. inches
5. inches 6. feet
7. inches 8. feet

Page 76
1. 6
2. 36
3. **Monster Movie**
4. 3
5. 6
6. 7

Page 77

Page 78
1. Aaron
2. Jenna
3. Tony
4. Jennifer
5. Manuel
6. Carmen

Page 79
1. C 2. E
3. F 4. A
5. D 6. B

Page 80
1. 342, 345, 348, 351, 354
2. 448, 460, 472, 484, 496
3. 507, 607, 707, 807, 907
4. 990, 987, 984, 981, 978
5. 740, 735, 730, 725, 720
6. 838, 842, 846, 850, 854

Page 81
Answers are correct when the following figures are circled:
1. first figure, showing $\frac{3}{4}$
2. second figure, showing $\frac{4}{8}$
3. second figure, showing $\frac{2}{3}$
4. second figure, showing $\frac{5}{6}$
5. first figure, showing $\frac{3}{4}$
6. first figure, showing $\frac{3}{3}$

Page 82
Combinations of dogs include:
Fido/Fluffy/Spike
Fido/Fluffy/Lou
Fluffy/Spike/Lou
Spike/Lou/Fido

Page 83

Most Likely	Least Likely
dime	quarter
nickel	dime
penny	dime
quarter	penny

Page 84
Rex; Mr. Wiggles; Foxy; Patsy; Sadie

Page 85
1. How many questions does Debbie have left to answer?
2. How many chapters does Gerard have left to read?
3. How many grocery items are there in all?
4. How many times does Irving brush his teeth in 4 days?

Page 86
The page is complete when the student draws each picture exactly without going over any line twice or lifting his or her pencil.

Page 87
1. combing your hair
2. making a pizza
3. playing a soccer game
4. reading a book
5. riding in an airplane

Page 88
1. 44 2. 24
3. 86 4. 2

Page 89
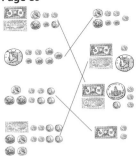

Page 90
1. Danny
2. Millie
3. Maria
4. Harry
5. Pete
6. Gabrielle

Page 91
1. 456 2. 1,027
3. 674 4. 865
5. 537 6. 4,356

Page 92
1. 551, 651, 751, 851, 951
2. 420, 410, 400, 390, 380
3. 45, 60, 75, 90, 105
4. 771, 769, 767, 765, 763
5. 845, 850, 855, 860, 865
6. Answers will vary.

Page 93
1. W, W, D, W, W, E, W, W
2. J, L, L, M, O, O, P, R
3. R, Q, P, O, N, M, L, K
4. E, E, E, E, E, F, F, F
5. O, O, P, Q, R, R, S, T

Page 94
1. $2.41
2. $1.54
3. 88 cents
4. $1.00
5. 43 cents

Page 95
1. spaghetti
2. $4.50
3. $3.75
4. $4.20

Page 96
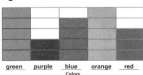
19 children voted

Page 97
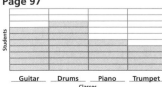

Page 98
1. 59 2. 12
3. 27 4. 68

Page 99
1. out 2. 11:30
3. 4:00 4. in

Page 100
The following shapes are circled:
1. square, octagon
2. trapezoid, hexagon, rectangle
3. trapezoid, triangle, parallelogram
4. hexagon, octagon
5. shapes with four sides

Page 101
1. dog
2. rabbit
3. giraffe
4. horse

Page 102
1. circle first figure, showing $\frac{2}{6}$
2. circle second figure, showing $\frac{1}{4}$
3. circle first figure, showing $\frac{1}{5}$
4. circle second figure, showing $\frac{2}{8}$
5. circle second figure, showing $\frac{2}{6}$
6. circle first figure, showing $\frac{2}{7}$

Page 103
1. $\frac{2}{2}$ 2. $\frac{2}{3}$
3. $\frac{3}{4}$ 4. $\frac{1}{2}$

Page 104
1. 8
2. 34
3. the 11th
4. 13

Page 105
1. +; − 2. +; +
3. −; − 4. −; +
5. +; − 6. +; +
7. −; + 8. −; −

Page 106
1. 96 − 75 = 21
   29 − 15 = 14
2. 50 − 10 = 40
   54 − 20 = 34
3. 77 − 55 = 22
   47 − 22 = 25
4. 68 − 32 = 36
   66 − 34 = 32

Page 107
1. 5,504; 5,506; 5,508
2. 30
3. 842
4. 84
5. 21

Page 108
1. 3,478; three thousand four hundred seventy-eight
2. 830; eight hundred thirty
3. 400; four hundred
4. 529; five hundred twenty-nine
5. 7,834; seven thousand eight hundred thirty-four
6. 4,052; four thousand fifty-two

Page 109
Combinations of leotard, tights, and skirt include:
pink/pink/pink
pink/pink/white
pink/white/pink
pink/white/white
white/white/white
white/white/pink
white/pink/white
white/pink/pink

Page 110
1. 73 + 11 = 84
    11 + 76 = 87
2. 46 − 22 = 24
    47 − 22 = 25
3. 15 + 23 = 38
    63 + 15 = 78
4. 73 − 52 = 21
    67 − 12 = 55

Page 111
1. 21
2. 23
3. 13
4. 131

Page 112

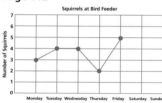

Page 113
1. $5.30
2. teddy bear and building blocks
3. toy robot and toy truck
4. $3.85

Page 114
1. pants and hat
2. pants
3. $4.60
4. pants and jacket

Page 115
1. measuring cup
2. ruler
3. scale
4. measuring cup
5. yardstick
6. ruler
7. scale
8. yardstick

Page 116
1. 8:00
2. 8:05
3. 8:25
4. 6 hours per day, 30 hours per week

Page 117
1. 164
2. 45 minutes
3. 11
4. 3

Page 118
1. 73 − 21 = 52
    56 − 34 = 22
2. 48 − 30 = 18
    84 − 64 = 20

3. 67 − 25 = 42
    66 − 45 = 21
4. 26 − 13 = 13
    96 − 81 = 15

Page 119
1. 5 x 2 = 10
2. 7 x 8 = 56
3. 3 x 4 = 12
4. 9 x 9 = 81
5. 4 x 7 = 28
6. 6 x 3 = 18

Page 120
1. Mrs. Hall
2. 2
3. Mr. Berkowitz
4. bar graph

Page 121
1. Museum
2. School
3. School
4. Park
5. Possible answer: Go to the start. Go right 4. Go up 2.

Page 122
1. 14   2. 84
3. 81   4. 13
5. 11   6. 17

Page 123
1. 8
2. 31
3. 28
4. 21

Page 124
1. 705 + 213 = 918
    513 + 182 = 695
2. 315 + 101 = 416
    308 + 610 = 918
3. 730 + 250 = 980
    626 + 150 = 776
4. 467 + 222 = 689
    254 + 421 = 675

Page 125
1. D   2. B
3. A   4. C
5. A

Page 126
1. 24
2. Sharie
3. Gerry
4. Gerry
5. Sharie
6. 4

Page 127
1. 15
2. 20 days
3. 26
4. 11 days
5. 4
6. 5

Page 128
1. 543 − 201 = 342
    423 − 301 = 122
2. 775 − 611 = 164
    918 − 805 = 113
3. 206 − 104 = 102
    732 − 531 = 201
4. 771 − 520 = 251
    477 − 126 = 351

Page 129
1. 7 x 7 = 49
2. 4 x 8 = 32
3. 8 x 5 = 40
4. 2 x 7 = 14
5. 9 x 2 = 18
6. 8 x 3 = 24

Page 130
1. 24   2. 21
3. 80   4. 27

Page 131
The following coins should be crossed out:
1. 1 half dollar, 1 quarter, 1 dime
2. 1 quarter
3. 1 quarter, 1 dime, 1 nickel, 1 penny
4. 1 dollar bill, 1 half dollar, 1 dime
5. 4 pennies

Page 132
1. 2:50; 10 minutes
2. 45 minutes
3. 10
4. 8 and a half hours

Page 133
1. inches
2. foot
3. feet
4. feet
5. inches
6. inches

Page 134
Answers may vary. Triangles drawn may include the following:
1.   2.

3.   4.

5.   6.

Page 135
1. pounds
2. ounces
3. ounces
4. pounds
5. ounces
6. ounces

Page 136
1. 10
2. Wednesday and Sunday
3. 56
4. 17
5. 8
6. Friday and Saturday

Page 137
Possible answers for questions 1–4 include:
3 half dollars
2 half dollars, 2 quarters
1 half dollar, 4 quarters
6 quarters

5. 15
6. 30

Page 138
1. 6 x 7 = 42
2. 6 x 6 = 36
3. 9 x 3 = 27
4. 2 x 6 = 12
5. 7 x 5 = 35
6. 6 x 9 = 54

Page 139
1. 63   2. 45
3. 20   4. $24

Page 140
1. 4   2. Thursday
3. 4   4. 3
5. 10

Page 141
Possible answers include:
1. Go right 1, go up 3.
2. Go right 2, go up 2.
3. Go right 3, go up 4.
4. Go right 4, go up 2.

Page 142
1. B   2. C
3. A   4. 8 cents
5. $1.47

Page 143
Possible answers include:
1. 1 dollar bill, 2 dimes, 2 pennies
    1 dollar bill, 4 nickels, 2 pennies
    4 quarters, 2 dimes, 2 pennies
2. 1 dollar bill, one half dollar
    1 dollar bill, 2 quarters
    3 half dollars
3. 1 dollar bill, 1 dime, 2 pennies
    1 dollar bill, 2 nickels, 2 pennies
    4 quarters, 1 dime, 2 pennies
4. 1 dollar bill, 1 quarter, 2 dimes, 1 penny
    1 dollar bill, 4 dimes, 1 nickel, 1 penny
    2 half dollars, 4 dimes, 1 nickel, 1 penny

Page 144
1. 51   2. 101
3. 86   4. Scott

Page 145
1. 7 x 3 = 21   2. 8 x 8 = 64
3. 4 x 6 = 24   4. 5 x 5 = 25
5. 6 x 8 = 48   6. 4 x 7 = 28

Page 146
1. 5
2. 11:30
3. 5
4. down
5. the bottom line

Page 147
Possible answers include:
1. Go right 1, go up 4.
2. Go right 2, go up 3.
3. Go right 3, go up 2.
4. Go right 4, go up 4.

Page 148
1. $\frac{1}{4}$ 2. $\frac{1}{3}$
3. $\frac{6}{12}$ 4. 4

Page 149

1.

2.

3.

4.

5.

6. The figure has no faces, and no vertices.

Page 150

Josh, Brendan, Mark, Jim, Craig

Page 151

1. 3 ounces
2. 28 pounds
3. 72 ounces
4. 26 pounds

Page 152

Possible answers for questions 1-6 include:
4 quarters, 1 dime
4 quarters, 2 nickels
3 quarters, 3 dimes, 1 nickel
2 quarters, 6 dimes
2 quarters, 5 dimes, 2 nickels
3 quarters, 2 dimes, 3 nickels

Page 153

Shirts should be colored with the following patterns:
1. red and white stripe, white and red stripe
2. yellow stars on an orange background, orange stars on a yellow background
3. blue and white striped, green and white striped
4. red, red

Page 154

1. 19 x 4 = ☐
2. 36 + 21 + 20 = ☐
3. 48 - 34 = ☐
4. 357 - 213 = ☐

Page 155

Plates should have the following combination of foods written on them:
sandwich/sandwich
soup/soup
salad/salad
stew/stew
sandwich/soup
sandwich/salad
sandwich/stew
soup/salad
soup/stew
stew/salad

Page 156

1. $\frac{3}{12}$ 2. $\frac{12}{24}$
3. 5   4. $\frac{2}{3}$

Page 157

Page 158

1. 100   2. cannot tell
3. 200   4. 100
5. 300

Page 159

1. 16   2. 24
3. 32   4. 15

Page 160

Clouds should have the following combinations of weather written on them:
sunny/windy
sunny/rainy
sunny/cold
windy/rainy
windy/cold
rainy/cold

Page 161

1. G, W, R, G, W, R, G, W
2. W, W, W, W, W, X, X, X
3. C, C, D, D, E, E, F, F
4. E, E, S, S, Y, Y, E, E
5. P, P, P, P, P, Q, Q, Q

Page 162

The following coins should be crossed out:
1. 1 dollar, 1 half dollar, 3 pennies
2. 2 dimes, 4 pennies
3. 1 dollar bill, 1 half dollar, 3 nickels, 2 pennies
4. 1 dollar bill, 3 dimes
5. 1 dime, 1 nickel, 1 penny

Page 163

The measurements of the lines are:
blue: 3 inches
red: 5 inches
orange: 4 inches
green: 2 inches
purple: 1 inch

Page 164

1. C   2. A
3. B   4. D

Page 165

1. 5 minutes
2. 25
3. 40
4. increasing with each grade

Page 166

1. C   2. A
3. B   4. B
5. A   6. A

Page 167

Most Likely	Least Likely
red	white
orange	red
green	yellow
blue	green

Page 168

1. 24   2. 63
3. 19   4. 11

Page 169

1. pen
2. sunglasses
3. baseball cap
4. mug

Page 170

1. 1 hour and 15 minutes
2. 3 days
3. 21 days
4. 55 minutes

Page 171

The colored backpacks include:
2 yellow backpacks
2 orange backpacks
1 red backpack
3 blue backpacks

Page 172

Answers will vary.

Page 173

1. X through trapezoid. The trapezoid does not have right angles.
2. X through parallelogram. The parallelogram has angles.
3. X through scalene triangle. The scalene triangle does not have a right angle.
4. X through square. The square has right angles and the other shapes do not.

Page 174

Answers will vary, but may include:
1. 1 half dollar, 1 quarter, 3 dimes
2. 2 half dollars, 1 quarter, 1 dime
3. 2 half dollars, 2 quarters, 3 dimes, 2 nickels
4. 3 half dollars

Page 175

1. 1 pound 13 ounces
2. 32 cards
3. 11 ounces
4. 16 pounds

Page 176

Kyle   Elena   Pedro
Hanna   Carter   Yoko

Page 177

Page 178

The following coins should be crossed out:
1. 1 dollar bill, 2 quarters, 1 dime, 1 nickel
2. 1 quarter, 1 nickel
3. 1 dollar bill, 1 half dollar, 1 quarter
4. 1 dollar bill, 1 quarter, 2 dimes, 2 pennies
5. 1 quarter, 1 dime, 1 penny

Page 179

1. carton
2. soup can
3. tissue box
4.

Page 180

1. 1:00   2. 1:45
3. 4:15   4. 6:00
5. 9:30   6. 11:45

Page 181

1. D   2. A
3. B   4. C

Page 182

The colored frogs include:
2 brown frogs
2 brown frogs with green spots
1 green frog with brown spots
3 solid green frogs

Page 183

1. magazine
2. tissues
3. orange juice
4. toy car

Page 184

1. 18   2. 12
3. 28   4. 24

Page 185

1. 7   2. 3
3. 6   4. 12

Page 186

1.   2.

3.   4.

Page 187

1. 88   2. 93
3. 72   4. 65
5. 54   6. 21